Fishing Alabama

Help Us Keep This Guide Up to Date

Every effort has been made by the author and editors to make this guide as accurate and useful as possible. However, many things can change after a guide is published—roads are detoured, phone numbers change, facilities come under new management, etc.

We would love to hear from you concerning your experiences with this guide and how you feel it could be improved and kept up to date. While we may not be able to respond to all comments and suggestions, we'll take them to heart and we'll also make certain to share them with the author. Please send your comments and suggestions to the following address:

The Globe Pequot Press
Reader Response/Editorial Department
P.O. Box 480
Guilford, CT 06437

Or you may e-mail us at:

editorial@GlobePequot.com

Thanks for your input, and happy fishing!

Fishing
Alabama

An Angler's Guide to 50 of the State's Prime Fishing Spots

ED MASHBURN

THE LYONS PRESS
GUILFORD, CONNECTICUT
AN IMPRINT OF THE GLOBE PEQUOT PRESS

The Lyons Press is an imprint of The Globe Pequot Press.

Photos by Ed Mashburn unless otherwise indicated.
Text design by Casey Shain
Maps by Tony Moore © Morris Book Publishing, LLC

Library of Congress Cataloging-in-Publication Data
Mashburn, Ed.
  Fishing Alabama : an angler's guide to 50 of the state's prime fishing spots / Ed Mashburn.
    p. cm.
  ISBN 978-1-59921-300-2
  1. Fishing—Alabama—Guidebooks. 2. Fishes—Alabama. I. Title.
  SH465.M37 2009
  799.109761--dc22

2008041274

Printed in the United States of America
10 9 8 7 6 5 4 3 2 1

Contents

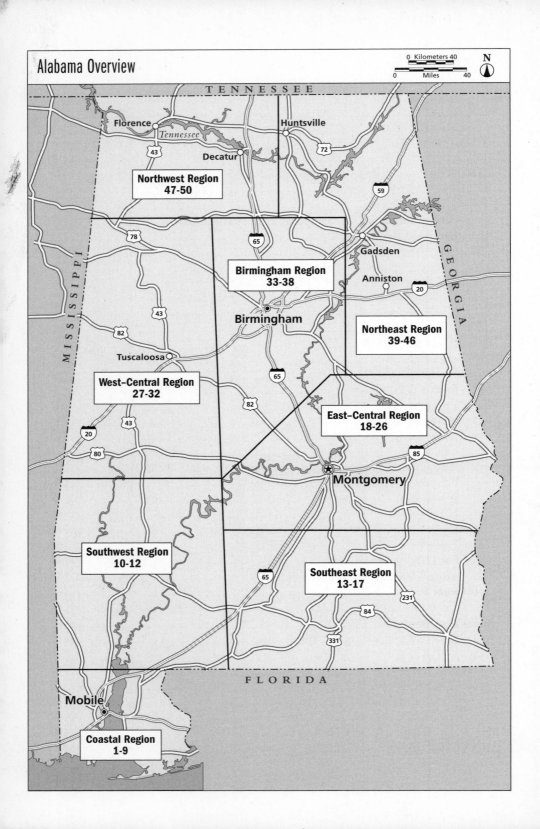

Alabama Overview

A fine misty morning makes for perfect west-central Alabama fishing conditions.

Acknowledgments

I would like to thank my daughter, Laurie, for guiding me through the computer-work of this book. I could not have written it without her help. I am blessed that my kids—Laurie, Fred, Dorothy, and Rob—will go fishing with me; I enjoy every trip with them. Without a doubt, my wife, June, is the best angler I fish with, and the source of all good in my life—my love and thanks to her. Finally, I would like to express my thanks to my father, who took me fishing when I was a child—it stuck with me.

Preface

One of the best things about writing a book is the fact that very often the writer learns much more from the field research than even the readers of the book. Such is very likely the case with this book. I have been fortunate to learn so much about my home state and the excellence and the tremendous scope of the fishing to be enjoyed here.

I would like to assure the reader of this book that I do not present myself as the final authority on "All Things To Do with Alabama Fishing." However, I am somebody who has spent a lifetime fishing in lots of different places, and I try to learn something new each time I go on the water. There is so much to be learned about fishing in Alabama that it would be impossible for one person to know it all, so please think of me as a fellow learner who observes and listens to those anglers who have far greater and wider knowledge, experience, and skill with fishing in this state. This book is my attempt to pass that knowledge along.

If I have any particular advantage over the average angler in Alabama that makes it possible for me to put this book together, it must be that my full-time work as a teacher in the Alabama public schools provides me with more time to spend on the water in pursuit of information, at least during the summer seasons.

I can't pretend that I have exhausted all possible places and techniques for great fishing in Alabama in this book. I've only scratched the surface, as I have come to realize from my research. However, I have tried very hard to present as wide a view of fishing in this state, from tiny mountain streams in the far north, to the large lakes in the middle parts of the state, to the vastness and wonder of the Alabama Gulf Coast waters. No doubt I have left many great fishing places out, but perhaps that may be corrected in the future.

It is my hope that anglers will enjoy this book, and perhaps be motivated to expand their own fishing experiences from something I have included in this book. I assure all, I have benefited very much from my work writing this book, and I hope to continue my research for many years.

Introduction

Anyone who is lucky enough to go fishing in Alabama will soon realize that he or she is in a good place. It really doesn't matter where in the state a person may be; good fishing is not far away. Alabama's major reservoirs and impoundments cover over a half-million acres. There are twenty-three smaller state-operated public fishing lakes scattered over the entire state. More than 77,000 miles of creeks, streams, and rivers offer fishing opportunities to anglers in Alabama. From the Appalachian Mountains and the Tennessee River Valley in the north to the swamps and bayous of the coastal south, Alabama anglers and Alabama fishing take a backseat to no one anywhere. The state is simply a great big fishing destination of world-class proportions. The hardest part of fishing in this state is selecting just what sort of fishing you want to do and where you want to do it.

The Alabama freshwater fishery, with its wide range of bass species, offers some of the best bass fishing in the world. The Crappie Capital of the World is located in Alabama, too. Countless smaller waters and huge impoundments produce panfish and catfish in abundance. Anglers can even catch the elusive rainbow trout in Alabama waters. Quite simply, there are many places to go fishing and many kinds of fish to catch in Alabama.

Although Alabama's Gulf coastline is limited in size, with only about 30 miles of actual coastline, some of the best saltwater fishing in the country is found here. Two first-rate marina and dock areas, Dauphin Island and Orange Beach, offer both resident and visiting anglers easy and safe access to the Gulf. Inshore saltwater anglers and offshore people alike can expect good and even great fishing from Alabama salt waters. Alabama has just about the best and most intense artificial reef construction program in the nation, and sport fishing benefits mightily from these reefs. Everything from highway wreckage to surplus army tanks to destroyed bridge materials have been placed on the bottom of the Alabama Gulf, where it attracts and holds a wide range of gamefish. For example, Alabama is red snapper central for the entire country, and anglers come from all over the nation and the world to fish for these beautiful and delicious reef-fish. Alabama's offshore Gulf waters produce large numbers of tuna, billfish, dolphin, and big mackerel every year.

An angler would have to look pretty far and wide to find another place that offers homefolks and visitors alike such a diversity of fishing possibilities. Before we look at specific places and specific fish to catch, there are some general topics we need to be familiar with.

Weather and Fishing

The two things cannot be separated. Fishing is greatly influenced by the weather. Anyone who has fished for long knows that often when the weather is awful, the fish really bite. Anglers can't always pick sunny, warm, pleasant days to fish.

However, it's no fun fishing when the angler is miserable from lack of proper protection. Alabama anglers, like anglers just about everywhere, must be aware of the weather going on and act accordingly.

Because Alabama's geography varies so widely, it is possible for the state to have cold, breezy, downright hazardous winter weather in the northern lakes and rivers while in the south and Gulf Coast, folks are fishing in shirtsleeves and shorts. Winter weather in particular can make selection of garments and protective gear quite a chore. When serious winter cold fronts blow through, Alabama anglers need serious protective garments, especially if riding in fast bass boats for extended runs. Even on the gentle Gulf Coast where it never gets very chilly for long, a cold front with wind and rain can make fishing unbearable if the angler is not prepared and dressed properly. Anglers in Alabama, especially in winter, should be dressed in layers so that clothing can be added or removed to match changing conditions.

Regardless of the season, the entire state of Alabama receives a great deal of rain, so anglers must be prepared for wet fishing conditions. Lightweight parka-type rain jackets that can be folded up into very compact bundles and stored on the boat or in a backpack are good things to have at any time. A head-to-foot lightweight rain suit is an even better idea. A light rain shower in the heat of summer can be refreshing and nice, but a downpour with wind, lightning, and torrential rain is no fun at any time. Getting wet in cold weather can be dangerous, not to mention miserable.

Spring weather in Alabama is often wonderful, but anglers must always keep in mind that a "Canada Clipper" cold front is always possible and that a cold wind can bring fishing to a complete halt. It seems that right around Easter nearly every year, a sharp cold front blows through and brings the spring fishing to a halt for a few days. Spring cold fronts never last long, but they can be unpleasant when they arrive. I can vividly remember shivering from the cruel north wind on a spring break trip to Lake Guntersville: I was too cold to fish because I was unprepared.

Summer weather in Alabama has its own set of considerations. Summer days in Alabama tend to be quite hot and humid and are often punctuated with violent afternoon thunderstorms. We can work around the heat and humidity by fishing early and late when the air and water are cooler, but when thunderheads pile up and thunder begins to rumble, anglers need to be careful. Trying to ride out a thunderstorm on a large lake or river is not wise. Winds can get quite violent, and lightning and water are not good together. Trying to ride out a thunderstorm on the open Gulf is always hazardous, and things out on the Gulf can get very bad. In addition to the normal dangers of thunderstorms, Gulf storms tend to produce water spouts: open ocean tornados. These little fellows are not the sort of thing anglers want to be involved with.

Autumn in Alabama can be grand. Along with football—we do enjoy football in this state, by the way—fishing is probably the most popular autumn activity for many, many residents and visitors. In general, autumn weather is the most settled of the year with cooler temperatures, fewer folks on the water, and fish feeding actively in preparation for winter. However, hurricanes come in the fall, and these terrible storms don't just affect the coast. When a hurricane comes ashore in Alabama, very often it creates storm conditions the entire breadth of the state. Storms in Birmingham and even farther north can be expected from hurricanes. When a hurricane is in the Gulf and approaching Alabama's coast, anglers should keep an eye and ear open to determine the probable path and take appropriate measures. Keep in mind that after a bad tropical storm passes, very often the finest weather of the whole year occurs, and very often fish bite very well, especially in the coastal areas.

Safety

Want to bring a promising fishing trip to a halt? Nothing beats a bad sunburn for putting the brakes on a fishing trip. Alabama's summer sun is intense, and even visitors who are well-tanned from their resident sunshine get badly burned when they come to Alabama unprepared. Both resident and visiting anglers should always use sunscreen and lots of it. The higher the ultraviolet protective rating, the better. The newer spray-on sunblocks are very convenient for anglers and don't require the angler to rub the sunscreen in the skin for protection (some sunscreens have an unpleasant taste for fish). Especially on the Gulf Coast where summer sun can be almost unbearable in the middle of the day, anglers should protect their skin. Hats, long pants in lightweight fabric, and long-sleeve shirts are all good. To our visitors on the Gulf Coast, I highly recommend timing your beach trips for early in the morning and late in the afternoon when the sun is not so brutally strong. The sun reflects off the white sand of the beaches, and it increases the probability of serious sunburn. This is no joking matter, especially for children.

A special mention must be made about sunglasses. A long day of super-bright summer sun is very hard on the eyes, and it can be harmful to long-term vision, so a good pair of sunglasses is a must. Of course, good polarized glasses have the additional benefit of cutting water surface glare and helping an angler spot a fish before the fish spots the angler. Putting on the 'glasses should be the first thing an angler does upon waking up each morning.

It should go without saying, but I can't let this chance to preach go by without mentioning personal floatation devices. I know that everyone understands not having a life preserver of some kind close at hand when on a boat is dumb. However, I also know that almost every angler who has been fishing for any length of time could tell stories of bad things that almost happened—or did happen—because of missing PFDs. This is particularly true for small children. Have an appropriate floatation device for each person, have it close, and when moving in the boat, have it on. There now, that's the sermon. (I will try to remember it myself when I'm fishing, too.)

Anglers in Alabama, especially river and stream anglers, have another concern. Be careful of strong currents. Be aware that current flow can change quickly, especially around navigation locks and dams. Also, fishing in tailrace waters below dams requires a great deal of attention. An angler wading in downstream waters must keep a constant vigilant eye on rapidly rising water. Very strong water flows can arrive with little or no warning. When fishing in the Gulf, tides can be very strong. Anglers need to be aware of this whether they are wading from the beach or fishing from a boat in the passes. Tides and boat wakes can take a wader's legs out from under him or her or put a small boat up on jetty rocks very quickly: Keep an eye open for what's going on around you.

Dangerous Critters

Along with weather conditions that can be challenging, anglers in Alabama must be vigilant when in the presence of wildlife. Some potentially dangerous animals make their homes either near the water or in it. When we go fishing, we may also be putting ourselves in the presence of the animals. However, just a little preparation and observation in most cases will either keep us from meeting potentially dangerous critters, or at least keep the danger to a minimum.

Bank anglers and wade anglers are at the most risk from critter encounters. Any time we go fishing from the land, we need to keep our eyes open because we're in "their" territory. Let's look at the most likely potentially dangerous animals we'll meet when fishing.

Snakes

Face it: They're out there, and some of them are very dangerous. Alabama is home to a wide range of snakes, and all of them orient to water at some time or other. Some poisonous snakes live in the water, so we've got to be aware of them. By wearing good footwear—high-topped wading boots are good—and especially watching where we step before we put our foot down, we can avoid most snake encounters.

In Alabama the most dangerous snakes likely to be encountered when fishing are cottonmouths. These are not nice snakes. They are quite poisonous, and they are not shy. This is one snake that may or may not back up when approached by a human. I have had cottonmouths approach me—out of curiosity, I believe—but it is quite unnerving when a big, thick, ugly cottonmouth comes close. By the way, the absolute best way in the world to get up close and personal with a cottonmouth is to drop caught fish on the bank behind you so you can get right back to the fishing. Cottonmouths will come to a flopping fish like little kids come to ice cream. When you are bank fishing, put caught fish on a stringer or in an ice chest immediately. No kidding: Letting fish flop on the bank is begging for trouble.

When fishing in thick timber, watch where you put your hands. Don't just reach over a fallen log either on the bank or out in the water. There may be something you really don't want to touch on the other side.

There are rattlesnakes in Alabama, and sometimes they will be found near water. Be especially snake-aware in dry times. Snakes will go to water when there is a drought, and they may not want to move for you. Most of the time, rattlesnakes will be away from fishing areas, but if you have to hike in to a creek or river, you may come up on a rattler. The best advice when dealing with a rattlesnake is to go around and give the snake plenty of room. When going around, watch where you step. For some reason, poisonous snakes are often found in small groups, so be careful when you see one snake. There may be another close at hand.

Finally, when dealing with snakes, keep in mind that snakebites in Alabama are almost never fatal. Please note that I didn't say they were fun. All reports I've read indicate poisonous snakebites hurt very much and make the bitten person quite sick. I have never been bitten, and by being careful, I plan to keep it that way!

Alligators

We share our lovely state with a large number of gators. Their numbers can range from being nonexistent in the northern lakes to being found just about every 50 feet or so on the banks of the Mobile Delta. Now, it is a shock for an angler to look around and see a 12-foot alligator sharing the same part of the lake or river. Trust me on this one, it *is* a shock; however, gators are not genetically programmed to see two-legged creatures that are the size of humans as potential food. Anglers run into trouble with gators for basically three reasons: One, the angler gets between momma gator and her nest or babies; two, the angler runs into a gator that has learned that humans feed them; and three, perhaps most dangerous of all, the angler has a dog along. This is serious: Gators don't see people as potential food, but Fido is a meal on paws. Every year many dogs are eaten by alligators in southern Alabama, and it's not a good way to see a family pet die. I wouldn't take a dog on a boat in the Mobile Delta or any of the southern Alabama rivers, and I absolutely would not take a dog on a bank fishing trip. Other than that, I really don't worry about alligators that much, and they are pretty cool to see.

Dangerous Saltwater Critters

Salt water presents a whole different range of potential animal problems for anglers. There are several things in the salt water that can hurt you. Probably the most common harmful critter in salt water is the jellyfish. There are many, many kinds of jellyfish, and some are no problem at all. Just the same, if you are wade fishing on the Gulf Coast and a Portuguese man o' war jellyfish comes in contact with you, you will discover a new meaning of pain. These terrible things hurt very much—it feels like fire—and it doesn't rub off. Jellyfish stings seem to hurt children even more than adults. Man o' war jellies are pretty easy to recognize; they are either purple or blue, and they float on the top of the water on what looks like an inflated purple sandwich bag. If an angler should come in contact with one—and there will be absolutely no doubt if it happens—the only thing to do is to immediately coat the stung area with unflavored meat tenderizer, just like you would put on a tough steak before cooking it. The meat tenderizer has an enzyme that neutralizes the stinging cells. I recommend all surf anglers buy and keep a small jar of meat tenderizer with them. Anglers, be aware that if you drag a fishing line against a man o' war and get some of the stinging tentacles on the line, if you touch the line, you'll get stung just the same as if the whole animal were there. These jellyfish are trouble, and sometimes they are thick in the water.

Another bad character in salt water that anglers have to be aware of is the stingray. These fish lie on the bottom, and if someone steps right on one, the fish may or may not inflict a very bad sting with a pencil-size barb that grows on top of its tail. Generally, if the ray does sting a person, the barbed stinger goes into the bone and then breaks off; the hospital emergency room is the next stop. Everything possible should be done to eliminate angler/stingray encounters. Anglers should not pick up their feet when wade fishing, but instead should shuffle their feet along to kick the ray before a foot comes down directly on it. Most serious stings happen when an angler backs up out of deeper water into shallow water or when an angler tries to remove a hook from a stingray to release it. Don't try to de-hook a stingray. Cut the line and let it go on its way.

Finally, possibly the most easily overlooked potential bad guy in salt water is the common oyster. That's right, the same guy you might have had a couple dozen of fried up and served with a few cold ones. How could an oyster hurt anyone? Well, he really can't, but his razor-sharp shell edges can. If a barefoot angler steps on an oyster shell—and the things grow everywhere in salt water that they can find a solid base to attach to—that angler's foot will be badly cut, and oyster cuts nearly always seem to get infected. Some very serious infections can be caused by oyster cuts. Saltwater anglers should wear good footwear, not flip-flops, when wade fishing.

Did you notice that I haven't talked about sharks? It's not because they aren't out there in the Gulf. They are, and in very great numbers, too. However, sharks are in much more danger from us than we are from them. Sharks will bite people, and when they do, it can be very bad. Most of the time, sharks just don't want to have anything to do with humans. In fact, most shark bites occur when an angler is trying to get a shark off a hook. The best way to avoid shark bite is to simply cut the fishing line and let the shark swim away. The bigger the shark, the farther up the line it should be cut. Do not try to remove a hook from a shark; that's chasing trouble fast. Cut the line and let it go.

Insects

Small critters can be the worst of all. I'm talking about bugs here. The state bird of Alabama ought to be the mosquito, because they are probably the most common flying creature in the state. Any angler anywhere in Alabama is subject to being bitten by mosquitoes. It goes without saying that anglers should use insect repellent, and in places where mosquitoes are particularly bad, anglers may have to resort to hats and headnets to keep the nasty biting things out of their eyes and noses. Long sleeves and long pants can help, but nothing seems to discourage the buzzing things for very long. I hate them.

Ticks and chiggers can be a problem in upland and wooded parts of Alabama. They don't seem to be nearly as thick in the southern parts of the state, and they are nonexistent on the coast. However, a hike through the woods to get to a fine bass creek in the Talladega Wilderness woods can collect an angler a fine batch of ticks. There are some pretty effective repellents on the market, and I would use them. How to get ticks and chiggers off? There are lots of ways to remove ticks, but the way I like best is to drive to the Gulf of Mexico and swim in the surf. The salt water kills them dead, and they fall off. It's true, I promise. It works for dogs, too.

To me, the worst of the bad small critters in Alabama are deerflies. I truly hate them. They can be found anywhere from the northern mountain lakes and streams to the beaches on the Gulf. They come in various sizes and colors—some have yellow heads and some have green—and when they bite, it hurts! I have found no good repellent, and they are too fast to slap. The only remedy I've found is to crank up the motor and speed away.

So that's about it for dangerous animals. There are bears in a few parts of Alabama, and a very few panthers, too. However, they pose no threat to anglers, and most anglers would consider themselves very lucky to get a glimpse of a wild bear or panther.

A little bit of care and attention should keep most potentially harmful angler-critter meetings from becoming a headline on the evening news.

Alabama Fishing Regulations

Basically it comes down to this: If you fish in Alabama, you will need a license if you are between the ages of sixteen and sixty-four. Annual fishing licenses are good for one year from the date of purchase; the prices listed here are for 2008. Alabama makes saltwater seven-day-trip licenses for seven consecutive days from date of purchase; this is a very handy option for vacationers. The annual saltwater license for residents is $16; the seven-day trip is $6, and the disabled angler license is $1.

For freshwater anglers, the annual license costs $9.50. By the way, the dividing line between freshwater and salt water is Interstate 10 in south Alabama. North of the interstate, you're in freshwater. South of the interstate, it's salt water. Combination fresh/saltwater licenses are available.

Licenses can be obtained online or by phone. To obtain specific details, anglers should contact the Department of Conservation and Natural Resources at (888) 848-6887.

Specific species limits and size restrictions can be obtained by contacting the Department of Conservation and Natural Resources. I didn't include specific limits for each species in this guide because these restrictions are changed by the authorities fairly often, especially in the Gulf of Mexico. Before going on a fishing trip, check online at the Outdoor Alabama Web site (www.outdooralabama.com) to obtain specific limits.

Alabama's Angler Recognition Program

Alabama has a number of programs that are designed to give acknowledgment to anglers who make significant catches of gamefish—records, in other words. The state has been maintaining records since the 1950s, and the process for recording the catch of record fish is really pretty simple. In order to be accepted as a new species record, a fish that weighs more than the current record must have its weighing on certified scales witnessed by two observers, the species must be identified by a state fisheries biologist, and there must be a side-view photograph. All rules and applications are available on the Outdoor Alabama Web site.

In addition to state records, there are also individual lake records for all four bass species (largemouth, smallmouth, spotted, and redeye). The potential record bass must meet the minimum weight requirements listed in the tables prepared by the state, have two witnesses of the weighing, be positively identified by a state biologist, and have a side-view photo. All applications for potential lake records must be returned within three months of the catch.

Master and Trophy Angler Certifications are made to honor folks who make an outstanding catch. Specific species requirements and guidelines are provided on the Master/Trophy Angler Recognition Form, which can be found on the Outdoor Alabama Web site. Other recognitions for these anglers are provided.

In addition to these programs, a Black Bass Grand Slam recognition is made to any angler who catches all four species of bass included in the program.

Although these recognition programs may seem by some to be a selfish attempt to gain attention for catching fish, the information provided by anglers who participate in the programs is invaluable to the state for planning and evaluation purposes. The general information is also presented to all anglers in the annual report from the Bass Anglers Information Team (BAIT).

Fishing Accessible to Everyone

Not everyone fishes the same way, and some anglers need a little extra help in order to put bait before the fish. Alabama tries to make sure that all anglers have access to fishing, even if this means that special provisions must be provided. The following sites are all wheelchair accessible: Wilson Dam, Fayette County Public Fishing Lake, Cedar Lake at Slickrock Pavilion, Lamar County Public Fishing Lake, Wheeler Lake at Mallard Creek TVA Day Use Area, Madison County Public Fishing Lake, Wheeler Refuge on pier off Highway 67, and Walker County Public Fishing Lake.

State Public Fishing Lakes

Most anglers think of Alabama's fishing in terms of major impoundments and rivers and even the Gulf of Mexico. In other words, BIG PLACES. However, not everyone can get to these major attractions, and to tell the truth, not everyone wants to go to these places. Many anglers seek out smaller, less crowded, lower-pressure fishing spots. The Alabama Wildlife and Freshwater Fisheries Division has just the answer for these folks.

Twenty-three public fishing lakes have been constructed in parts of the state where natural fishing waters are either hard to reach or just not present. All of these lakes, which range in size from 13 to 184 acres, are stocked with largemouth bass, bluegill, redear sunfish, and channel catfish. Crappie have been stocked in addition to these species in several of the public lakes. Hybrid striped bass and even rainbow trout have been stocked in certain lakes.

Operating hours can change, but most public fishing lakes are open six or seven days each week from February to December. Many of the lakes are closed from December 1 until the end of January for maintenance and stocking. Please check specific lake managers to confirm fishing times.

These state-operated fishing lakes are great places to take kids or older folks for easy in-easy out fishing. Also, they are great places for us to practice new fishing techniques in real-world situations. We might need a place on the water to practice our fly-casting, for example, where catching a trophy is not as important as perfecting a skill, and perhaps catching a fish while we develop a skill is still a possibility.

Anyway, these are nice waters to go for a good day's fishing. For more information, visit www.outdooralabama.com/fishing/freshwater/where/lakes.

Locations and Contact Numbers of Public Fishing Lakes

Barbour County Lake near Clayton: (334) 775-7123
Bibb County Lake near Centreville: (205) 938-2124
Chambers County Lake near Lafayette: (334) 864-8145
Clay County Lake near Delta: (256) 488-0038
Coffee County Lake near Elba: (334) 897-8212
Crenshaw County Lake near Luverne: (334) 335-2572
Dale County Lake near Ozark: (334) 774-0588
Dallas County Lake near Selma: (334) 874-8804
DeKalb County Lake near Sylvania: (256) 657-3000
Escambia County Lake near Brewton: (251) 809-0068
Fayette County Lake near Fayette: (205) 932-6548
Geneva County Lakes near Enterprise: (334) 684-9434
Lamar County Lake near Vernon: (205) 695-8640
Lee County Lake near Opelika: (334) 749-1275
Madison County Lake near Huntsville (trout fishing from Thanksgiving until March): (256) 776-4905
Marion County Lake near Guin: (205) 921-7856
Monroe County Lake near Beatrice: (251) 789-2104
Pike County Lake near Troy: (334) 484-9610
Walker County Lake near Jasper: (205) 221-1801
Washington County Lake near Millry: (251) 846-2512

How to Use This Guide

I have made every effort to keep this guide as simple and easy to use as possible. I have tried to present as much information as possible about specific gamefish and places to fish for them without loading the pages down with needless words. Here's the way this guide is designed to work.

In the individual site descriptions, I've tried to represent the different regions of Alabama as fairly as I could. There are so many great places to fish here, and so many different ways to fish, some locations just had to be left out. What follows is an explanation of how each site description is organized.

Each site description starts with a **Key species** section that lists the most commonly caught gamefish in that location. Following that, an **Overview** section includes a brief summary of the area, followed by a more detailed **Description** section. **The fishing** section goes into more detail about equipment, lures, technique, and other specifics. That is followed by a section that provides page numbers and grids that allow you to locate specific sites by referring to DeLorme's excellent *Alabama Atlas & Gazetteer* (found at any bookstore). This atlas is a great resource for any angler who wishes to do a little paper exploring. A **Camping** section provides information to the closest facilities. Of course, preference was given to public campground and parks, but when public facilities are not present, private locations are given. **Tips and cautions** includes insider advice or safety warnings. **Directions** are given from larger cities and intersections to make driving and towing a boat easier. Most sites in this guidebook can be driven to in street vehicles; no sites that require off-road vehicles are listed. Finally, the **For more information** section directs anglers to sources of further information. Complete contact information for these agencies and organizations can be found in the appendix.

Final Comments

There are so many fine places in Alabama to fish that anglers might come to think of Alabama as having unlimited fishing and unlimited fishing locations, and therefore, no care of the water or shoreline should be needed. This is far from true. All of Alabama's fishing water needs and deserves constant attention and diligence from anglers. For instance, anglers must be careful to not just wad up and toss old fishing line into the water or shoreline. I know, we all get in a hurry to fish and want to clear our reels so we can make the next cast, but we can't just throw old line away. Discarded fishing line can become a death trap for wildlife. All trash looks bad, and it can be hazardous to waders and boaters. Garbage dumped into creeks and rivers is unforgivable. Anglers must be at the forefront in the struggle to keep our waters and shorelines clean.

Apparently, Alabama is inhabited by a large tribe of yahoos who think that any stream, river, or lake exists to provide them a disposal place for their trash. It is infuriating for an angler to visit a beautiful fishing spot only to find someone has dumped several loads of trash in the creek. We anglers can do a couple of things in this situation: One, walk on past and try to ignore the mess; or two, try to pack at least a little bit of the mess away to proper disposal sites. I'd like to suggest to all of us anglers that choice number 2 is our best bet to maintain our streams and lakes in their best condition.

Another final comment I would like to make to my fellow anglers is that we all need to try to include our younger family members in our fishing lives. Little kids have trouble being quiet. Little kids don't really see much difference between that five-pound bass you think you can catch and a pint-size bluegill, but taking kids fishing can be some of the best time ever spent with them. I fished with all of my kids when they were small, and those trips are some of the best memories I have. Parents, remember that these same little kids who you introduce to fishing when they are small are the same people who may take you fishing when they get older. Also, I have not heard of many teenagers getting in much serious trouble while they were fishing. As a parent and a teacher for a long time, I think that if more parents took their kids fishing, there would be fewer incidents of trouble for the police to handle.

Alabama State Records

Let's look at the range of state record fish caught in Alabama's waters—it's an impressive list of big fish.

Freshwater Records

Bass, Hybrid	25 lbs. 15 oz.	Drum, Freshwater	41 lbs. 8 oz.
Bass, Largemouth	16 lbs. 8 oz.	Eel, American	5 lb. 8 oz.
Bass, Redeye	3 lbs. 2 oz.	Gar, Alligator	151 lbs. 5 oz.
Bass, Rock	1 lb. 6 oz.	Gar, Longnose	32 lbs. 14 oz.
Bass, Shoal	6 lbs. 11 oz.	Gar, Spotted	8 lbs. 12 oz.
Bass, Smallmouth	10 lbs. 8 oz.	Muskellunge	19 lbs. 8 oz.
Bass, Spotted	8 lbs. 12 oz.	Paddlefish	52 lbs. 12 oz.
Bass, Striped	55 lbs.	Perch, Yellow	1 lb. 15 oz.
Bass, White	4 lbs. 9 oz.	Pickerel, Chain	6 lbs. 5 oz.
Bass, Yellow	2 lbs. 8 oz.	Pickerel, Redfin	6 oz.
Bowfin	18 lbs. 6oz.	Redhorse, Silver	14 lbs. 14 oz.
Buffalo	57 lbs.	Sauger	5 lbs. 2 oz.
Bullhead	3 lbs. 13 oz.	Sunfish, Bluegill	4 lbs. 12 oz.
Carp	35 lbs.	Sunfish, Green	1 lb. 9 oz.
Carp, Grass	70 lbs.	Sunfish, Longear	8 oz.
Catfish, Blue	111 lbs.	Sunfish, Redbreast	13 oz.
Catfish, Channel	40 lbs.	Sunfish, Redear	4 lbs. 4 oz.
Catfish, Flathead	80 lbs.	Trout, Rainbow	7 lbs. 4 oz.
Catfish, White	10 lbs. 9 oz.	Walleye	10 lbs. 14 oz.
Crappie, Black	4 lbs. 5 oz.	Warmouth	1 lb. 12 oz.
Crappie, White	4 lbs. 9 oz.		

Saltwater Records

Amberjack	127 lbs. 12 oz.	Crevalle, Jack	39 lbs. 4 oz.
Angelfish, Blue	2 lbs. 3 oz.	Croaker, Atlantic	4 lbs.
Barracuda	52 lbs. 4 oz.	Dolphinfish	60 lbs.
Barrelfish	12 lbs.	Drum, Black	61 lbs.
Bass, Longtail	5 lbs. 10 oz.	Drum, Red	43 lbs.
Bass, Striped	55 lbs.	Escolar	62 lbs. 7 oz.
Bigeye	3 lbs. 2 oz.	Filefish	8 lbs. 8 oz.
Bluefish	17 lbs. 4 oz.	Flounder, Southern	13 lbs. 3 oz.
Bonito	5 lbs. 5 oz.	Grouper, Black	63 lbs. 1 oz.
Brotula, Bearded	19 lbs. 8 oz.	Grouper, Gag	74 lbs. 8 oz.
Catfish, Gafftop	8 lbs. 13 oz.	Grouper, Red	34 lbs. 10 oz.
Catfish, Sea	2 lbs. 15 oz.	Grouper, Scamp	29 lbs. 10 oz.
Chub, Bermuda	10 lbs. 5 oz.	Grouper, Snowy	52 lbs. 9 oz.
Chub, Yellow	7 lbs. 4 oz.	Grouper, Warsaw	226 lbs.
Cobia	117 lbs. 7 oz.	Grouper, Yellowedge	46 lbs. 8 oz.
Creolefish	13 oz.	Hake, Southern	6 lbs. 4.5 oz.

Hind, Red	2 lbs. 14 oz.	Sharksucker	4 lbs. 7 oz.
Hind, Speckled	22 lbs. 14 oz.	Sheepshead	12 lbs. 15 oz.
Jack, Almaco	47 lbs. 8 oz.	Snapper, Cubera	52 lbs.
Kingfish (Whiting)	2 lbs. 15 oz.	Snapper, Dog	13 lbs. 4 oz.
Ladyfish	4 lbs. 8 oz.	Snapper, Gray	15 lbs. 11 oz.
Little Tunny	21 lbs.	Snapper, Lane	7 lbs.
Lookdown	2 lbs. 2 oz.	Snapper, Mutton	13 lbs. 12 oz.
Mackerel, King	67 lbs. 15 oz.	Snapper, Red	44 lbs. 12 oz.
Mackerel, Spanish	8 lbs. 12 oz.	Snapper, Silk	6 lbs. 3 oz.
Marlin, Blue	779 lbs. 5 oz.	Snapper, Vermillion	7 lbs. 3 oz.
Marlin, White	98 lbs. 13 oz.	Spadefish	6 lbs. 12 oz.
Moonfish	1 lb.	Spearfish, Longbill	53 lbs.
Mullet, Striped	1 lb. 2 oz.	Squirrelfish	1 lb. 1 oz.
Pinfish	3 lbs. 2 oz.	Stargazer, Southern	6 lbs. 4.5 oz.
Pompano, African	38 lbs. 7 oz.	Stingray, Roughtail	160 lbs.
Pompano, Florida	5 lbs. 8 oz.	Stingray, Southern	125 lbs.
Porgy, Red	7 lbs. 6 oz.	Swordfish	350 lbs. 12 oz.
Porgy, Whitebone	7 lbs. 6 oz.	Tarpon	203 lbs.
Puffer, Smooth	3 lbs. 10 oz.	Tilefish, Blue	6 lbs. 12 oz.
Rosefish, Blackbelly	2 lbs. 8 oz.	Tilefish, Northern	26 lbs. 3 oz.
Runner, Rainbow	19 lbs. 9 oz.	Toadfish, Leopard	2 lbs. 13 oz.
Runner, Blue	11 lbs. 2 oz.	Triggerfish, Gray	13 lbs. 8 oz.
Sailfish, Atlantic	81 lbs.	Triggerfish, Queen	7 lbs. 8 oz.
Seabass, Black	3 lbs. 2 oz.	Tripletail	37 lbs. 5 oz.
Searobin, Blackwing	1 lb. 13 oz.	Tuna, Bigeye	51 lbs. 14 oz.
Seatrout, Spotted	12 lbs. 4 oz.	Tuna, Blackfin	32 lbs. 12 oz.
Seatrout, Sand	6 lbs. 11 oz.	Tuna, Bluefin	829 lbs. 6 oz.
Shark, Atlantic Sharpnose	16 lbs. 3 oz.	Tuna, Skipjack	29 lbs. 8 oz.
Shark, Lemon	278 lbs. 8 oz.	Tuna, Yellowfin	221 lbs. 7.2 oz.
Shark, Mako	737 lbs.	Wahoo	123 lbs. 6 oz.
Shark, Tiger	988 lbs. 8 oz.	Wreckfish	68 lbs. 6 oz.

Common Fish Species of Alabama

This section provides specific information about the most commonly encountered gamefish in the state. It is designed to give anglers a quick overview of the specific fish, where they live, how they live, and how to catch them. Fieldmarks for identification of specific fish are provided, and specific cautions and other species-specific information is also given. If I have left out a favorite fish in this guide, I apologize. Especially in the salt water, there are just too many fish to examine in detail.

The **Best bet** section at the end of each specific species' listing gives anglers the locations where the species is usually found in large enough numbers to make the fishing effort for it worthwhile. However, anglers must keep in mind that fish can and do move around, and that sometimes they just aren't where they are supposed to be.

Freshwater Fish Species

Bluegill bream

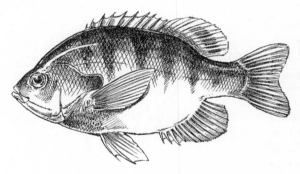

Sunfish tend to be "circular" in shape, and big ones are just about as high as they are long. Bluegills follow this pattern. Big ones, up to three pounds in some cases, are quite thick and round. Big bluegills have beautiful dark overall coloration with purple hues on their sides, and very often yellow or orange bellies. They have a light blue tint to their lower jaws and gill covers, hence the name. Bluegills have a tendency to reproduce rapidly, and without constant removal of bluegills either by anglers or larger predatory fish, they will quickly overpopulate a body of water. Thankfully, lots of things in and around the water love to eat bluegills, and anglers should, too. Bluegill make first-rate table fare, and a bunch of bluegills cleaned and fried up right make a great meal.

Casting: A fairly light rod and reel combination should work well for these tough-fighting panfish. A 6-foot light action rod and reel with six-pound line will be adequate for bluegill bream unless fishing in very brushy or obstructed areas. Most anglers will choose to use a spinning rig simply because it is easier to use and cast lighter weight lures and baits than level-wind reels.

Bluegill will actively strike a wide range of artificial lures. In-line spinners in smaller sizes work well. Smaller jigs in either feather, hair, or soft plastic tails will attract a bluegill's attention. These jigs should be worked rather slowly toward the bottom of the water around cover. However, for the most fun, very small top-water lures such as Rapalas and tiny Rebels cast near shoreline cover will result in some very violent strikes from bluegills. Bluegills will almost always find a top-water lure irresistible, and they will sometimes hit lures much too large for them to eat.

Bait fishing: Most bluegills are caught on live bait cast near shoreline cover such as lily pads, blown-down trees, brush piles, and cypress trees. Small gold hooks with extra-long shafts to make hook removal easier are the standard baitfishing setup. Thread a fat worm or lively cricket on this hook, drop it near cover, and hold on! Bluegills will take such live bait very actively. Some anglers prefer to fish live bait under small bobbers while other anglers insist on simply tight-lining the live bait as it naturally sinks toward the bottom. Either way will work very well.

Fly fishing: This is probably the ultimate fun way to catch bluegill. A small yellow or black popping bug cast near shallow water cover will tempt hungry bluegills. Bluegills will attack these small top-water bugs with gusto, and they often hit as the bug lies motionless. Although popping bugs are the standard fly lure, bluegills will readily take sinking patterns. Wooly buggers and other "suggestive" insect patterns will take bluegills, but so will the traditional rubber-legged "bream killer" sinking fly. Again, bluegill will take surprisingly big offerings, so don't feel compelled to offer up tiny flies. Bluegills like a good mouthful of food.

Best bets: Look for shoreline cover in the spring, summer, and fall. The bream will be close to cover most of the time. As weather cools in the winter, bluegill will leave the shoreline shallow and head to deeper water. Bluegills will be found in huge lakes, small ponds, major rivers in the backwaters and sloughs off the main channels, and in creeks and streams. In fact, just about anywhere there is fresh water of any decent quality, bluegill will be there.

Crappie, black and white

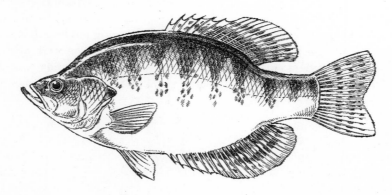

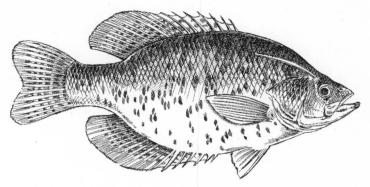

I've combined the two species of crappie found in Alabama because they really are very similar. Except for biologists, probably no one is too interested in whether a particular crappie is white or black, and they all eat the same, which is very well. The crappie is one of the very best freshwater fish for the table, with firm, delicate white flesh. In appearance, crappie are fairly robust fish and are considerably "taller" than they are thick; they can be quite thin after spawning. They are covered with black spots on a basic silver background. They have fairly large mouths, but the tissue of the mouth is very thin, and hooks tear out easily. Crappie are not great fighters when hooked, and they will never challenge a bass to a pulling contest. However, the large numbers of crappie that can be caught at times and the great eating they provide make crappie probably the second most popular gamefish in Alabama after the bass family. Crappie are very prolific in Alabama, and Lake Weiss is known as the "Crappie Capitol of the World." All of the larger lakes and rivers hold good populations of crappie, and in the springtime, getting a bucket of minnows and some light tackle to go after a mess of crappie is an Alabama tradition. Oh, yes. The name can be pronounced "CRAP ee" or "CROP ee." Either name will work

Casting: Fairly light tackle—6- to 7-foot spinning rods with matching reels—will work well. However, when fishing especially for crappie, the line needs to be a bit heavier than most people would expect; ten to fifteen pound is good. This is not because the fish demand such heavy line, but because crappie love to school up in and around heavy brush cover, and hang-ups are inevitable. With the heavier line, an angler can pull the thin wire hooks used for crappie fishing straight out of a snag without breaking the heavier line. Otherwise, a crappie angler will be retying hooks and lures all day long. Crappie will almost always be near heavy cover when they spawn in the spring, so look for brush piles and tree tops in the water to start the search for crappie. Artificials will work for crappie if they look like minnows. Small light-colored jigs and little Beetlespin lures will take crappie. They almost never take top-water lures.

Bait fishing: This is the ticket for a full ice chest. In the spring at any bait shop near a major lake or river in Alabama, anglers will be able to buy a bucket of crappie min-nows—2- to 3-inch-long shiners—and this will do for a day's fishing. Most crappie experts use bobbers to help suspend the minnow near cover. It is just as effective to

Introduction

tight-line a crappie minnow on a single gold hook with a small split shot to take it down near cover. Watch the bobber and watch the line! Crappie are very good at removing bait minnows from hooks with just the slightest movement of the line.

Fly fishing: I have seen crappie caught on fly rods, but it is rare. I expect a light-colored streamer fished deep near shoreline cover would work, but it would be a lot of trouble.

Best bets: Any of the big reservoirs and rivers in Alabama hold massive populations of crappie, but Lake Weiss is best.

Rainbow trout

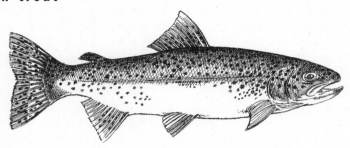

Nearly every fish, with the possible exception of gar, is attractive in some way or other, but the rainbow trout has a large share of attractive qualities. They are elongated fish, their fins are soft with no sharp spines, and their smooth skin is usually well-dotted on the top and sides with deep, black spots. However, on the sides of the fish is their namesake, the rainbow. This varies from fish to fish, but almost all rainbow trout have a wide band of bright pink to bright red on their sides. Fish fresh from the hatchery tend to be duller in coloration, but after a few months in the wild, their colors tend to deepen and grow more intense. A rainbow trout that has been living in the wild and eating wild food for a year or two is a truly beautiful animal. Rainbow trout are very active fighters when hooked, also. Nearly every trout will jump repeatedly and make strong runs with rapid changes of direction when they feel the pressure of a hook. Many hooked rainbows leap themselves free from hooks, to the angler's frustration.

Casting: Most folks who fish for rainbow trout in Alabama use ultra-light spinning gear. A light rod, about 5.5 to 6 feet long, is good. Rigs using four- to six-pound line are just about right. By setting the drag light and giving a hooked fish plenty of time to tire out, surprisingly big trout can be caught. The idea is to have a rig that can cast a light lure or single hook baited with live bait a long way. Trout have very good eyes, and too much movement on the shoreline will spook them. Most trout in Alabama will run about a foot long and perhaps a pound and half in weight, so this light gear will be just about right.

Artificial lures sometimes work well on 'Bama's trout. Small in-line spinners such as Roostertails and Mepps will catch trout, especially in low-light situations.

These spinners should be worked slowly. Cast out across the stream, and retrieve the spinner just fast enough to make the blade spin; don't make the bait look like a torpedo! If you can see the lure from across the stream as it spins toward you, it's going too fast.

One of my favorite trout lures is a tiny, 1/16- to 1/32-ounce dark-colored jig. Either traditional bucktail or feather tails will work, but so will soft plastic bodies. I cast this little jig as far as I can, and then let it settle to the bottom. I then try to swim the jig back in tiny little hops across the bottom. I lose some jigs sometimes, but I also have hooked my largest trout this way. When a hungry rainbow grabs a jig fished this way, he usually hits it pretty hard.

Bait fishing: If you're serious about catching a rainbow trout in Alabama, live bait is the way to go. Red worms and crickets will work. Use a small gold hook and just enough split shot to help cast, and pitch the bait into a deep pocket. Most trout caught on live bait come from deeper, slower water with just a bit of current.

Commercially prepared trout baits work very well. They come in horrible-looking colors such as super-bright pink and Day-Glo chartreuse, but the trout seem to like them just fine. Berkley makes some very effective trout bait: Their products are called Power bait and Power eggs, and these products are sold at larger sporting goods stores and local trout-stream bait shops.

Believe it or not, trout will bite such things as small balls of Velveeta cheese molded around a hook and whole kernels of canned corn.

Fly fishing: This is the classic fishing technique for trout. Most Alabama trout fly anglers use fairly light fly rods; four-weight or five-weight work just fine. In the one trout stream of Alabama, the Sipsey Fork below Smith Lake Dam, fly anglers use tiny midge imitation flies in mostly dark colors with just a flash of color. These little bugs look much like the midges, which hatch on a daily basis from the waters of the lake. These tiny flies can be hard to fish mainly because they are hard to track in the water, but they are very effective.

Best bets: There's really just one game in town. In Alabama the only flowing trout stream open to the public is the Sipsey Fork. However, that's not so bad. Trout have been caught in this river up to 50 miles downstream from the dam, so there's lots of water to fish.

Redeye bass

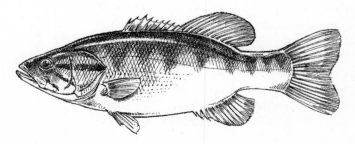

This is a gorgeous little bass, both for its appearance and for its habitat. In many ways, the redeye looks very similar to a spotted bass, but its mouth is just a bit smaller, and its eyes are, indeed, quite red. A good fieldmark to identify the redeye bass is that in most individuals, the tail fin will be outlined with a white band. As far as their habitat goes, these are creek and stream fish, and almost never are caught in lakes or reservoirs. They seem to be located mainly in the Tennessee River and Coosa River drainages. They prefer clear, clean water with lots of rocks and boulders.

Redeye bass don't get too big—a three-pounder is a very good fish—but a fish that size hooked in fast-running creek water is a great deal of fun. They tend to lie in deeper pools that are close to fast-moving water, and they like boulders to hide behind. Catching a redeye bass is a good sign of a creek or stream being in good shape. These fish will not tolerate pollution or poor water quality.

Casting: Light spinning gear is best for these small battlers. A 5- to 6-foot light spinning rod and reel to match with six- to eight-pound test line will be just about right. Tackle heavier than this will only cut down on the chances of catching one of these wary, wild fish. In clear, low-water summer conditions, anglers may have to scale back line weight to six-pound or even lighter.

Redeyes can be taken on small, dark colored in-line spinners such as Rooster-tails. I like the red and orange colors since these suggest crawfish, which are one of the redeye's favorite natural foods. Small dark plastic worms on 1/8-ounce jig heads are good, too. Redeyes will take top-water lures when the light is low, but they prefer underwater lures. I like to let a lure drift downstream with the current when fishing for redeyes. Especially when fishing a jig and plastic worm tail, I let the lure go all the way to the bottom and try to hop it back across current. This often draws hard strikes from redeyes, which are down deep in the cool, dark water.

Bait fishing: Make it crawfish! A small 1- to 2-inch crawfish hooked through the tail and tossed in the shadow of boulders in creek pools is the best way to catch a redeye. They will take other live baits—worms, crickets, grasshoppers—but the creek bream usually beat the bass to these baits.

Fly fishing: The long rod is great fun for redeyes. A fairly lightweight rod—three to four weight would be fine—and larger dark streamers and other underwater bugs work fine when worked slowly through the deeper pockets of a creek. Popping bugs cast under overhanging limbs is exciting; this will catch anything in the creek, including redeyes.

Best bets: On the map (Delorme is a great map source), look for rivers that drain into Lakes Guntersville, Wheeler, Weiss, and Martin. Most of these creeks will have redeye bass in them. Look for county road crossings on the map, and then go explore.

Spotted bass

This is a very attractive fish. It follows the basic largemouth bass color scheme, but spotted bass seem to have stronger, more well-defined patterns. The side band is quite pronounced and is more a series of dark blotches than a unified band. The mouth of spotted bass does not usually extend past the eye as largemouth bass mouths do, but this is not a reliable identification mark. Spotted bass are found in all of the larger impoundments north of Montgomery, and in some lakes they are the dominant bass species. These bass seem to be better suited for life in deep, clear, rocky-bottomed lakes than largemouth. Spotted bass do not grow quite as big as largemouth, but six-pound and larger spots show up fairly often. Spotted bass tend to be very aggressive feeders, and when schooling up in open water, they can boil the water as they feed on shad. Spotted bass seem to prefer shad as primary forage, but they will not turn down a crawfish. Spotted bass seem to be just a little bit quicker, more aggressive, and more determined than largemouth bass when they inhabit the same body of water.

Casting: Medium weight and action spinning and casting rigs work well for spots. Six- to 7-foot rods with eight- to twelve-pound line will do nicely. The heavier line would be needed when fishing heavy cover such as bluffs, boulders, and underwater logs. Sometimes, long casts are needed to get lures before spooky spots, and this is where the lighter line comes in handy. Spots respond very well to soft plastic baits in either white/silver or dark crawfish patterns fished along steep shoreline drop-offs. Either traditional jigheads or slider type jigheads work well. The size of lures needs to be scaled down just a bit for spotted bass. They like the same stuff as largemouth, just not quite as big. Spinner baits in silver and chartreuse can produce lots of spotted bass, especially in the spring. Top-water lures will take spotted bass, especially when they are taking shad in open water. Don't be afraid to let a top-water lure sit still for long time when fishing for spots. They don't always hit the bait when it's moving.

Bait fishing: Live shad will attract spotted bass, as will crawfish fished near deep bluffs and boulders. Also, a live crawfish fished near mid-lake rises and hilltops that come up to 12 or 15 feet from the surface will catch spots. In rivers and streams, crawfish will take a great many spotted bass when fished in deeper pools and pockets.

Fly fishing: Anglers in larger streams are discovering how much fun a four-pound spotted bass can be when caught on a fly rod. Four- to five-weight rods and rigs are just about right. Especially in the Coosa River below Jordan Dam, fly fishing for spots is becoming very popular. Fly anglers should work fairly large, dark streamers and crawfish imitations in the deeper holes.

Best bets: All of the northern lakes and rivers hold spotted bass. For best big spots, anglers should try Lake Martin, Lake Smith—some huge spots are there—and Lake Wheeler.

Channel catfish

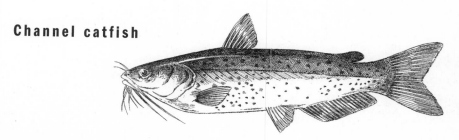

This is the classic catfish in form and function. It is a slim, trim, streamlined fish, at least in its younger days, but as it grows older and larger—and it can grow pretty large—a big belly develops, and much of the streamlining is lost. It has a basic steel blue and silver color pattern, which shades to a white belly. Small spots are very often found on the tail and fins. As individual channel catfish grow larger, the color tends to be a solid dark gray with the white belly. Like all catfish, there are no scales but a smooth, slick skin. Most channel catfish caught in Alabama weigh less than ten pounds, but anglers should know that in some of the larger lakes, and especially the larger rivers, channel catfish can and do grow to weigh more than one hundred pounds. These are massive fish, and they are not easy to catch. All channel catfish give a good account of themselves when hooked, and the big fish seem to know where every snag and obstruction on the bottom is located so they can tangle lines and break free. The state of Alabama stocks thousands of catfish in the various public waters of the state, and this is the fish that is commercially grown on catfish farms throughout the South. We eat lots of channel catfish fillets down here in the South. Hooking this fish is not as easy as anglers might think. Channel cats have a tendency to nibble a bait, sometimes for a long time, before they take it deep enough to be hooked. Anglers sometimes have to show a lot of patience before trying to set the hook on channel cats. Like most catfish, channel catfish prefer a little current, and in the major rivers where they grow to such large sizes, if no water is flowing, the catfish usually don't bite. When catching channel catfish, anglers should exercise care when unhooking the fish. They have a tendency to roll over violently both when they are in the water and when they have been caught. This can put the angler at risk of being finned, and catfish fins hurt a great deal when they puncture an angler's hand!

Casting: For smaller "fiddler" channel cats of less than ten pounds, a medium-action rod and reel combination will work fine. About a 7-foot rod and a reel with fifteen-pound test line does well. Either spinning or level-wind casting rigs are good, but I prefer the level-wind reel because these reel drags tend to be better and less likely to lock up when a bigger than usual channel catfish makes a strong run. As the size and weight of catfish increases, so must the tackle. If an angler targets standard river-run channel cats (these can be from ten to thirty-five pounds, generally), then a rig capable of using fifty-pound line and two-ounce or larger weights will work. If the truly monster catfish of seventy-five pounds or more are being sought, then deep-sea fishing rigs that use one-hundred-pound line and rigging are in order. Of course, we don't get to "special order" the size of our catfish, and sometimes one of the big ones shows up when we are rigged for the smaller fish. The usual result of this kind of encounter is a reel stripped of line, and a fish story of the "one that got away" type. A wise catfish angler will tend to "overgun" in the weight of line and rig, just in case the big one shows up.

Although channel catfish do take artificial lures (usually a soft plastic bait worked slowly on the bottom for largemouth bass), this is not common.

Bait fishing: Such a wide variety of live baits are used for channel catfish that anglers might think catfish will eat anything as long as it has scent and seems alive. Well, that's right, they will. Channel catfish are caught on dead shrimp, raw chicken livers, cheese baits, blood baits, live minnows, dead minnows, crickets, red worms, and even chunks of Ivory soap! Many commercially prepared catfish "stink" baits are sold, and they all work. My personal favorite channel catfish bait is a large, late-July size yellow grasshopper. I put one of these on a stout hook, drop it in a deep pool, and if Mr. Whiskers is there, he will take it. A very good bait for channel catfish in the larger sizes is a fresh-caught bream of about hand-size. These bream are the channel catfish's natural food, and a lively bream on a heavy hook and rig sent to the deepest part of a river where a little current is flowing around a logjam or rock piles will usually attract a big catfish. The rest is up to the angler. For the very biggest catfish, in the huge lakes and rivers, large live shad are the ticket. Hook up a live shad, cast it into the fast tailrace waters of the big dams, and hold on!

Fly fishing: Since channel catfish rarely take artificials of any kind, fly casting is not a common technique. However, I had an uncle who used live bait, crickets usually, on a fly rod, and he caught a great many channel catfish. He was a singular man with set ways.

Best bets: Channel catfish are found statewide, and just about any freshwater lake or stream will have good populations. For the very biggest catfish, try Lake Wheeler, Lake Wilson, and Lake Guntersville. For river fishing, the Alabama River from Montgomery south to the Mobile Delta is good. The Conecuh River in southeastern Alabama is a famous catfish stream: lots of catfish, and some big ones are there, too.

Largemouth bass

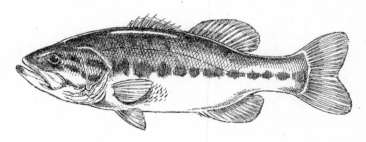

This is the star. This is one of the most famous species of fish in the world. Each year, millions of dollars and millions of hours are spent by anglers in pursuit of this fish. Bass tournaments with lots of money and television coverage going to winners are held on nearly every summer weekend somewhere in the state. Several big-business industries from boat manufacturing to companies in the fishing tackle line spend and make millions of dollars every year designing and producing artificial lures and tackle just for the capture of largemouth bass. This fish is a very important individual in the world of fishing.

Largemouth bass are elongated fish, and like people, they tend to be thinner and more streamlined in the smaller, younger ages, and then become thicker and more robust as they get older. Largemouth bass are very aggressive predators, and they will eat just about anything that will fit in their mouths. In Alabama largemouth bass weighing up to fifteen pounds and more have been caught. However, most largemouth bass caught here will be in the two- to six-pound range. They do have big mouths, which, when closed completely, extend past the eye of the fish. This is a classic identification tool: If the mouth goes past the eye of the fish, it's a largemouth. Coloration can vary widely. In most cases, largemouth bass are almost black on top, shading to green on the sides, with bellies almost white. A pronounced dark band will almost always be found extending down the fish's side. However, largemouth bass caught in very cloudy or muddy water can be an almost uniform pale tan color, almost white.

When hooked, largemouth bass almost always jump. Some hooked bass seem to spend more time in the air than pulling against the line in the water. Although the jumping is very exciting for anglers, bass can pull very hard when they decide to go the other way. Probably more big bass are lost when they pull free or make it to underwater cover where they can tangle the line and get free rather than from their jumping. Big bass seem to know where all cover is located in their home areas, and they use this cover to maintain their freedom.

Largemouth bass are found in lakes, streams, ponds, and rivers all over the state of Alabama. From the clear, fast-moving creeks of the Tennessee River Valley to the brackish marshes of the Gulf Coast, largemouth bass will be found. They tend to prefer deeper, slower-moving water with underwater structure close at hand, but they can and will be found in almost all freshwater locations from time to time.

Casting: Bass gear can range from light spinning rods in the 5.5-foot range and six-pound test line to 6-foot rods with thirty-pound test line and heavy duty level-wind casting reels. It all depends on the size of fish being sought. In lakes and ponds where big bass live—and big ones can live in some pretty small ponds—heavier tackle should be used. For serious bass anglers, twelve-pound test is a good compromise. It is strong enough to handle most bass, yet it is light enough to enable anglers to cast effectively lighter lures.

It is up to individual anglers whether to use spinning or casting reels. I prefer spinning reels for most occasions when I go bass fishing, but when I go BIG bass fishing, I like casting reels with their better drag systems. Of course, my biggest bass have all come on spinning rods and reels, and I was lucky to get the big fish in.

As far as selecting bass lures, anglers face a daunting challenge. There are thousands of artificial lures designed for bass, and they all work at certain times. However, for day-in/day-out use, it is hard to beat subsurface soft plastic baits. These baits can be worm shaped, crawfish shaped, or have no definite shape at all. Some soft plastic baits have scents added to attract fish, while others don't. Each bass angler will develop his or her personal preferences. My son, Rob, likes white soft plastic jerk baits, while I prefer crawfish-colored plastic worms. We both catch fish on our choice of plastic baits. Many bass are caught on spinner baits. These things don't look like anything that ever lived or swam. However, bass love them, and at certain times of the year, spinner baits are deadly on big bass. My favorite colors are gold and black and chartreuse. Finally come top-water lures. There is nothing in the fishing world to compare to the sight, sound, and feel of a bass as it crashes a top-water lure. It is addictive. Although it is probably not the most reliable way to catch bass, it is no doubt the most fun. Oddly enough, all of my larger bass have come on top-water baits. I prefer a top-water bait with spinners; two classics are the Devil's Horse and the Torpedo lures. My biggest bass—she was about ten pounds—came on a Torpedo lure cast near a brush pile this spring. I'll remember that strike and fight until I die.

Bait fishing: Many, many bass are caught on live baits. Many are caught by mistake: The angler was fishing for something else and a bass just happened to take the bait. Bass will eat crappie minnows, and they will also take big gobs of worms meant for catfish. In my opinion, the best live bait for big bass is a live crawfish hooked through the tail and allowed to drift down toward underwater logs, boulders, or brush piles. Bass love crawfish and will almost never turn one down.

Fly fishing: This is a fishing technique that is really gaining in popularity, especially in the northern parts of the state where some first-rate wading and floating streams have good largemouth bass populations. Good success can be had with light- to medium-weight fly rods and fairly large popping bugs cast under shoreline vegetation. A popping bug dropped in the shadows below overhanging tree limbs is a wonderful way to catch bass, and some pretty big bass will rise to poppers in this situation. Stream largemouth bass are often caught on large, dark-colored underwater flies. Dark streamers and Wooly Buggers will take largemouth. Of course, a three-pound largemouth hooked on fly gear will put up a struggle not to be forgotten.

Best bets: The entire state of Alabama is largemouth bass country. From streams to massive lakes to big rivers to bayous and swamps, and, of course, private lakes and ponds, the star of Alabama freshwater fishing will be there.

Redear bream

This attractive bream is typically bream-shaped, which means it is basically just about as high as it is long, especially in the mature fish. Its coloration tends to be dark green to black on the very back of the fish, and the sides tend to be mottled silver with greenish and black markings on the sides. However, the giveaway for identifying this fish is to look at its gill flap. The true redear will have a bright red flap from its gill covers. No other bream has this feature. Redears grow to respectable sizes, especially for bream. Two-pound redears are common, and four-pounders aren't that rare. They eat a wide range of food, but they are very fond of freshwater shellfish; hence their common nickname, "shellcrackers." Redears are delicious and, being larger than most bream, are easier to clean and prepare.

Casting: Many redears are taken on cane poles and worms, so equipment is not crucial. For the most fun, and these hefty bream are a lot of fun to catch, a light spinning rod with perhaps six- or eight-pound line works very well. Since these bream don't seem to hold quite as tight to cover as many other bream species, they can often be hooked and played in open water where the lighter line used will not be such a handicap. I have caught some very nice redears on small Beetle Spin lures and other spinners intended for bass. These bream tend to bed in the spring a little deeper than most bream, so anglers looking specifically for redears might want to try fishing a bit slower and deeper than for bluegills, for example. Small jigs worked slowly along the bottom catch redears. These bream are not as eager to hit top-water lures as most bream species are. They will take a bug from the surface, but they seem to prefer eating subsurface.

Bait fishing: Most redears are taken by anglers who drop a worm or cricket to the bottom and let it sit there. Live bait is by far the most productive way to gather an ice chest of fat redears for a fish fry. A big gob of redworms on a hook in about 6 feet of water is in prime territory for redears to find and chow down on.

Fly fishing: Redears are taken on flies, especially in creeks and rivers. Wooly Buggers in dark colors and medium sizes work especially well when the fly is allowed to drift with the current in deeper water near logs, boulders, and other deeper water structure. Four- to five-weight fly rods are just about right for redears.

Best bets: Although redears do inhabit many creeks and streams from the far northern borders of Alabama to the bayous of the Delta, the largest individuals tend to come from lakes that have good populations of shellfish, crawfish, and insect larvae. Lake Guntersville, Lake Weiss, and some of the Coosa River lakes are good places to catch redears in the larger sizes. For just numbers of fish, most of the rivers and streams of the state will have good populations of redears.

Smallmouth bass

I might as well confess the truth right now. Smallmouth bass are my favorite freshwater fish. I'd rather catch one smallmouth than ten bass of any other kind. Smallmouth bass fight harder, jump more, and pull stronger than any other freshwater fish pound for pound. I also love the places where smallmouth live: clear creeks and streams, clear, deep rocky lakes, places with good quality water. Smallmouth bass tend to be a more uniform pattern and color than other bass species. The dark band along their side is not nearly as strong and pronounced as on largemouth or spotted bass. Also, instead of green as the basic color, smallmouth tend to be brown, darker on top and lighter on bottom. The best way to recognize smallmouth bass is to look at their mouths. When pushed closed, smallmouth bass mouths end well before the position of their eyes. Also, smallmouth bass often have redeyes, but this is not consistent. Anglers in Alabama are lucky to live in a place where world-record smallmouth bass live. Up in the northern parts of the state, particularly in the Tennessee River drainage and the big lakes created by the damming of the river, smallmouth bass grow big and mean, and there are lots of them. These bass love current, and smart anglers will use that to target smallmouth. Places where big rocks break the current and create slack water are perfect places to cast for smallmouth.

Casting: For stream smallmouth bass, anglers should use light- to medium-weight spinning gear. Six-foot rods with matching reels and eight-pound test line are just about right for most situations. A good drag system needs to be in working order. For smaller creeks, lightweight spinning gear is a lot of fun. In creeks and streams, anglers would be wise to use artificial lures that resemble crawfish. Small (one-eigth to one-fourth ounce) jig heads with soft plastic bodies in brown or green colors with orange trim work great. Fish these around big boulders and deep pockets. I also recommend small floating/diving minnow imitations in gold colors that can be cast under tree limbs into shadow areas. Smallmouth will rise up and smash these offerings.

For lake and major river situations, which is where the world-record fish come from, anglers will need twelve- or fifteen-pound test line and either good quality spinning or level-wind reels. When fishing for big smallmouth in the tailrace situation below dams, anglers will need to use silver and other shad-colored lures—spoons, jigs, spinner baits—to target these fish. Be prepared to get hung and lose some lures on the rocks, but also be prepared to hook some of the biggest smallmouth bass in the world!

Bait fishing: In smaller water, live crawfish are the best bait for smallmouth bass. Hook a crawfish (2 to 3 inches long is a good size) and toss it near deeper cover and hang on. If a smallmouth is there, he will eat the crawfish. Minnows seined out of a creek can also be effective, but crawfish are the best bet.

For the big waters of lakes and major rivers, live shad are the best baits. Hook these through the lips or back and put just enough weight on to take the shad down. Try to keep the bait out of the rocks, but it has to be close enough to draw the attention of the smallmouth. Keep a tight line, and be ready for some tremendous strikes. There should be no doubt at all when a big smallmouth takes the shad bait!

Fly fishing: Fly anglers in the northern parts of the state have scouted out some great little smallmouth streams, but they are petty close-mouthed about their locations, and I don't blame them. These little creeks won't stand much pressure from overfishing. However, look on the DeLorme maps, and see where creeks enter into the Tennessee River lakes. These are possibilities. Creek smallmouth like to hit subsurface flies such as Muddlers, Wooly Buggers, and any streamer tied thick and in dark colors to resemble a crawfish. Fish these deep and near rocks; try to keep the line tight. Small poppers cast under tree limbs can be a great deal of fun.

Best bets: The biggest smallmouth bass will be caught below the dams at Lake Wheeler, Lake Wilson, and Lake Pickwick. These are big, strong waters, so anglers need to be careful. A guide is a good idea for the first trip or two.

Striped bass, white bass, and hybrid striped bass

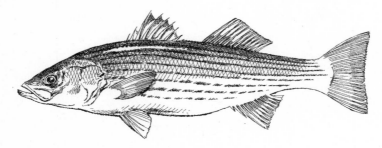

I've combined these three fine sport fishes because even though there are important differences in the species, they are in fact closely related, and when anglers catch one of the species, chances are the other species are close at hand, too. These are all very strong fish. A hooked three-pound white bass pulls very hard, with frequent changes of direction, and whites don't tire quickly. A hybrid bass does the same stuff, but it weighs twice as much as a white bass. A striper does the same thing, too, but some stripers weigh thirty pounds or more! A big striper hooked in fast current is a handful for any angler, and most really big ones don't stay hooked long; they are just too strong. The only fish of this group native to the entire state of Alabama is the white bass. Stripers have been stocked in larger reservoirs and rivers, and the hybrid was created in hatcheries by crossing the smaller white bass with the much larger striped bass. All of these strong pullers are basically open-water fish, and they are shad-eating machines. Most lakes in Alabama have very heavy populations of shad, and without these white, hybrid, and especially the striped bass eating up lots of the shad, the lakes would soon become overpopulated with oversize shad that largemouth and spotted bass can't eat. A thirty- or forty-pound striper can eat some pretty big shad! Anglers who go out for these fish should keep in mind at all times that shad is the fish to imitate. Artificial lures should be white, chrome, chartreuse, or combinations of these colors. Lures that can be cast long distances, such as spoons and jigs, are good. During the spring, all of these fish make runs up creeks and rivers to spawn, and they almost always are stopped by dams that block their progress. Anglers who fish live shad or shad imitation lures in the waters below these dams can have fantastic catches of these strong fish. During the warmer and cooler seasons, all of these fish tend to stay in the deeper water of the open lakes and rivers. In color and pattern, these three species are quite similar. Dark black lines or broken lines are on the sides, while the basic coloration is a chrome-silver with darker backs and white bellies. These are some nice-looking fish. Be careful when unhooking these fish! They have some very sharp edges to their gill covers, and they will cut up a hand very quickly and very badly. Wear gloves, or in the case of big stripers, use a lip-gripper to lift the fish into the boat or on shore.

Casting: When fishing for any of these fish, pretty heavy tackle is needed, mainly because an angler never knows when a big striper will show up and take a lure or bait intended for a three-pound white bass. Six- to 7-foot medium to heavy spinning and casting rods with matching reels and twenty-pound line will work. When specifically targeting big stripers, thirty-pound line is not too heavy, and I would recommend a good saltwater-quality level-wind casting reel and matching rod. These are some BIG fish, and patience will be required to land a large one of any of these species.

Bait fishing: A trophy striped bass fishery has developed in Smith Lake where big live shad are dropped to schools of big stripers in deep water. This is a very effective technique when targeting stripers. Most of the time live bait is not needed to tempt either whites, hybrids, or stripers. However, when this is needed, anglers should try to match the live bait being offered to the predominant size food fish in the lake at that time.

Fly fishing: Guides offer trips for fly anglers to go after stripers in the spring in some of the larger lakes. This will take heavy tackle: seven- to eight-weight rods and matching rig. Both angler and guide need to be prepared to crank up the motor and chase down a strong striper on a fly rod if it decides to run downstream for a long way. Flies should resemble shad, and they should be allowed to sink fairly deep in the current. Stripers and hybrids are caught fairly often during the later spring and summer in the larger rivers and streams of central and northern Alabama by anglers fishing primarily for spotted and largemouth bass.

Best bets: Any of the large lakes and rivers, but Smith Lake is probably the best bet with Wheeler and Wilson not far behind.

Saltwater Fish Species

Amberjack

The only way a land-bound angler or tourist will see the purely offshore amberjack is when another angler who has been out in deep water brings one to the dock. Amberjack are large fish when mature; fish approaching and passing one hundred pounds are found on the deeper offshore reefs and gas drilling rigs. AJs, as they as popularly known by anglers, are elongated fish with large mouths and a dark "eye mask," which is a good field mark for identifying the fish. Their coloration is a basic

Amberjack are very hard work.

dark brown on top, shading to a lighter amber-brown on the sides, to white on the belly. The best way to correctly identify an amberjack is to look at the angler who just caught the fish. If the angler is running with sweat, rubbing sore muscles, and asking to sit down for a while, then he or she probably just caught an amberjack. All Gulf fish pull hard, but AJs are in a class by themselves. Amberjack have the well-deserved reputation of being just about the longest-lasting, hardest-pulling, never-to-give-up fish in the water. They are good eating when in the smaller sizes (twenty pounds or less), and blackened amberjack is a classic Gulf Coast meal. These are deep-water fish, and mature individuals will rarely be caught in less than 100 feet of water. They also tend to orient to reefs, wrecks, and other offshore hard structure.

Casting: Heavy big-game rigs capable of handling very strong fifty-pound or bigger fish should be used when seeking AJs. Anything less and the fight will be very short as the fish will immediately overpower the equipment and run into the wreck or reef and hang up the line and break off. Smaller amberjack (twenty pounds or less) can be caught on heavy spinning gear, but the spinning gear needs to be stout enough to handle the constant pressure that a hooked AJ puts on gear and angler. An angler needs to have a fighting belt to help control the fish and limit the pressure that the hooked fish puts on the angler. Fifty-pound line and even heavier leaders are needed, and fairly large circle hooks are best. Amberjack will hit a wide range of artificial lures. Heavy jigs with or without a tipping of live fish or chunk of dead bait will work. Heavy spoons in silver and chrome finishes hook a lot of amberjack. Recently, Gulf Coast offshore anglers have had very good success on AJs with "butterfly spoons" and matching rigs. These are Japanese imports that have unusual hook and rigging setups but are apparently very successful.

Bait fishing: Most amberjack are caught on live bait. Many times, rigs sent down for snapper and grouper are instead taken by AJs, which occupy the same sort of reef terrain the other fish prefer. Amberjack will eat live bait (cigar minnows, menhaden, pinfish), but they will also take frozen or fresh dead bait, too. Chumming for amberjack can provide some very fast and furious offshore action when the fish are willing to leave their reef locations down deep and follow the trail of fresh scent up to the surface. When this happens, anglers can sometimes use considerably lighter tackle than when the fish are deeper and closer to the safety of the reef or wreck. For the very biggest amberjack, anglers using very heavy gear will send a blue-runner of a pound or more on a big circle hook down deep toward the reef. When the big ones hit, the angler had better be ready for a long, hard battle.

Fly fishing: Just about the only way a fly angler could hope to meet up with an amberjack would be when chumming a reef to bring the fish up to shallower water. In this case, a large, light-colored streamer or popper might just attract a strike. After that, it's all up to the angler to try to hold on!

Best bets: An angler would need either a private boat or a charter captain to go out to the deeper reefs. Any of the 100- to 200-foot reefs will usually have a population of amberjack. For the very biggest AJs, head to the offshore gas rigs; the Petronius is a good place to start.

Dolphin

This is a gorgeous, almost indescribable fish. Bright neon greens, blues, golds, and stripes and spots all play over the skin of this fish as it chases its prey through the blue waters of the open Gulf of Mexico. A super-fast growing fish, dolphin can gain more than five pounds in the first year or so of life, and a twenty-pound fish may be only a couple of years old. They don't live long—five years is about the maximum age—but in that time they may grow to seventy pounds or more. Dolphins have another oddity about them: Males and females look very different from each other. Mature male dolphins have a very high, blunt forehead while the females have a more rounded, "normal" looking head. Dolphin bodies are compressed so that they

A small dolphin that took a live bait.

are very thin, but very high vertically. Most dolphins caught in Alabama offshore waters weigh between ten and thirty pounds, but eighty-five-pound fish and bigger do show up from time to time. Some very big dolphins are caught offshore around the gas rigs. Smaller dolphins are caught as close to shore as a mile or less off the beach. They are very active predators, and they are fast enough to catch flying fish when they reenter the water after a long flight to escape predators. When a dolphin is caught, its colors flare and then fade out to a uniform gray, mottled color as the fish dies. The colors somewhat return after death.

Casting: Fishing for dolphin can be a lightweight game, or it can require big-game tackle. For most "schoolie"-size dolphin, up to about twenty pounds, medium-heavy spinning gear with twenty-pound test line and a heavier leader will work well. Level-wind casting gear is likewise suitable. A 6.5- to 7-foot rod that has some backbone to it is best. Long casts may be required, or the fish may be directly below the boat. It is very difficult to pattern dolphin. Most dolphins that are caught on artificial lures hit spoons and trolling heads intended for king mackerel or wahoo. Smaller-size dolphin (ten pounds or so) like to hit one-half to one ounce light-colored jigs. Dolphins like to hang around floating objects—tree trunks, mats of floating Sargassum weed, anything that floats—and anglers often use these floating objects to help locate schools of dolphin. For "bull" dolphin (fish of fifty pounds or more), heavy big-game equipment such as is found on charter boats is needed. Forty- to fifty-pound lines and heavier leaders are used on these big fish.

Bait fishing: Dolphins are very susceptible to live bait. Cigar minnows (live or dead), menhaden, and small Spanish mackerel will all attract the attention of dolphin. When a school of dolphin is located—and they are almost always found in schools—live bait chopped up in the water to make a chum will help excite the dolphins and keep them in the vicinity of the boat. A chunk of live bait on a strong, medium-size hook drifting back away from the boat in the chum line is probably the best way to hook up with a dolphin.

Fly fishing: Now this is fun! Saltwater anglers have discovered the excitement of hooking and catching dolphin on the long rod. Smaller dolphin, up to about ten pounds, can be effectively worked on five- to six-weight rods. Any bigger than ten pounds, eight-weight or larger fly rods will be required. The super-heavyweight fish—fifty pounds and more—will need maximum fly gear. Big Clousers and light-colored Deceivers will attract the attention of dolphins, as will any large fly that looks alive in the water. Most fly anglers rely on a chum line to attract the dolphin close enough to the boat for casting.

Best bets: Most serious dolphin anglers start their search for these brilliant fish 20 miles or more offshore in the summer time. These are warm-water fish, and they don't show up nearly as much during winter months. The farther offshore the fishing is done, the better chance for bigger fish. Using a guide from Dauphin Island or Orange Beach would be the best idea to learn how to target and reach these wonderful game fish, at least for the first few trips.

Grouper (gag)

There are a number of different species of grouper in the Alabama Gulf waters, but the most common and a good representative fish is the gag grouper. This is a robust fish with a shape very much like a huge largemouth bass. In color, gag grouper have a basic dark brown, and they very often have mottled patterns of lighter brown that shade to a white belly. The mouth is very large with some very impressive sharp teeth. Gag grouper can get large; twenty-pounders are common on the offshore reefs. Grouper are structure-oriented fish and almost never are found away from some sort of reef, wreck, hole, or piling. Grouper are first-rate eating fish. They fillet out very well, and either fried, grilled, blackened, or baked are very good. Gags will provide a hard fight when hooked, not in the same league with an amberjack of equal weight, but a good fight nevertheless. Small gag grouper are often caught inshore around pass bridges and other inshore structure. These pretty little fish show all of the same habits as their larger offshore relatives.

Casting: Most gag grouper are caught offshore using heavy level-wind reels and matching heavy duty rods. Fifty-pound line and heavier should be used to help keep these strong fish coming up when hooked and not heading back into the reef where they will certainly tangle the line and get free. Grouper can sometimes be chummed up from the deep water and when that happens, they can be caught on lighter spinning gear—twenty- to thirty-pound line will work. Grouper will hit heavy jigs lowered to reef structure and hopped along the bottom, but they like the jig to be tipped with some sort of live bait.

Gag grouper are great fun to catch and great on the plate!

Bait fishing: By far, the largest number and largest size gag grouper are caught on live bait. Gags are not picky, and just about any live bait lowered in their territory will draw a strike. I prefer a big, hand-size or larger, pinfish hooked on a circle hook through both lips and lowered to just above the reef structure. The strike is usually not long in coming. Cigar minnows, menhaden, and fresh-caught squirrel fish or ruby-mouth grunts are very good live bait for gags.

Fly fishing: I've never heard of anyone catching a gag grouper on fly gear. It might happen if they were chummed to the surface, but it would be highly unusual.

Best bets: Any of the state reefs hold gag grouper, and they would be good places to start looking. Better fish come from 150-foot or deeper water, and the very biggest gags will be around the far offshore drilling rigs.

Redfish

This is my favorite inshore fish (also known as red drum, rat reds, or bull reds). I treasure redfish for their willingness to bite a wide range of offerings and for their wide range of sizes. I've caught fine little half-pound "puppies" in small canals and backwaters that fought hard for their size. I've also caught thirty-five-pound mature fish in the Gulf that fought me to a standstill for more than thirty minutes before I finally won the battle. These are serious hard-pulling fish. Although they have the name "redfish," more often than not these fish will be a silvery color, but sometimes they do have a gorgeous copper-colored hue, especially if they come from clear waters. Regardless of the overall coloration, all redfish will have one, or sometimes more than one, very dark black spot near the tail. This is an absolute certain field-mark for identifying redfish. Redfish will live in the open Gulf, and they will also live far up freshwater rivers; they are very adaptable to salinity levels. Because of large-scale commercial fishing, redfish stocks were pushed very low in the late 1980s and 1990s. However, because of severe limits and size restrictions placed on the fish, populations have rebounded very well, and now there are plenty of reds to go around for sport anglers. In addition to their absolutely first-class fighting abilities and willingness to bite a variety of baits, smaller redfish, say five to six pounds and in the slot size for keeping, are some of the best eating fish in the Gulf. They fillet up easily and cleanly and are delicious. I do love these old redfish!

Casting: Selecting tackle for redfish will depend on the size fish being sought. For five-pound "puppy" reds, medium-action spinning or light casting rods of about 6 feet in length and matching reels will work nicely. For bigger "schoolie" reds of ten to fifteen pounds, a rod and reel combination that will hold fifteen-pound test line works well. For the big breeder-size fish in the Gulf and passes, most of the time no more than twenty-pound line will work if the reel's drag is up to the job. Anglers who want to specialize in fishing for reds will want to invest in a reel with a very good, very reliable drag system because reds will tax a reel. They make very long runs, and they are tough to slow down, much less stop. Reds will bite a wide range of artificial baits ranging from deep-diving lipped plugs to top-water "walk the dog" lures to big bass-type spinner baits worked around inshore cover. The most reliable lure for reds is a one-ounce jig with a scented plastic tail. When the big pass reds are chasing bait, an angler can throw this lure a long way to reach the feeding fish. Color doesn't seem to be too important, but I like my jig and tail lures to have at least a flash of white somewhere on the bait.

Bait fishing: Reds will bite a wide range of live baits, and anglers are not seriously limited in the choice of live baits reds will take. Live crabs drifted with the current through the Gulf passes will take the big reds. Cut bait and dead pogies or cigar minnows will take reds. Inshore, reds will take bull minnows and other small fish. Without a doubt, no matter the situation, the best redfish bait is live shrimp. I've caught little babies and thirty-five-pound mommas on the same size live shrimp. A live shrimp hooked under the horn on its head and allowed to free-line with the tide is the best way to hook a redfish. When a redfish takes a live shrimp, there will be no doubt at all; the strike will be hard and sudden, and the battle will be intense. Anglers using live bait for reds should always use circle hooks, which cut down on the occurrence of gut hooking, which almost always results in a dead fish when the fish is released. Make certain the hook is up to the job: Thin wire hooks will be straightened out by big reds going the other way.

Fly fishing: Although not many fly anglers target reds, this technique is growing more popular all the time. Fly anglers work inshore flats and reefs and cast shrimp imitation and large Deceiver-type flies to attract feeding reds. Top-water flies will also work when the reds are in a chasing mood; poppers and gurglers will do fine. Medium-weight fly rigs of six- to seven-weight and fifteen-pound leaders will work, and anglers should be able to make long casts to reach targeted fish.

Best bets: For smaller reds, any of the feeder rivers that empty into Mobile Bay are good bets. For the big reds, Dixie Bar is one of the best places in the world to catch twenty-pound-plus redfish. Year-round fishing for reds is the rule; they never leave our coastline entirely.

Sheepshead

This is perhaps the easiest inshore fish to identify. Bold black and white vertical stripes with a mouthful of "clown teeth" means you've caught a sheepshead. A very robust fish, with prominent pectoral fins and large, rough scales, sheepshead are very common in Alabama inshore waters. They love hard structure such as dock pilings, bridge abutments, oyster reefs, and boat wreckage, where they use their large buckteeth to nip off barnacles and other shellfish. They have seasonal migrations that take huge numbers of these fish from their summer and winter home in the bays and rivers surrounding Mobile Bay and Perdido Bay and other inshore areas to the passes leading into the Gulf, where they spawn in early spring. Sheepshead can be caught year-round, but most of them are caught during the late winter/ early spring spawning runs. Massive schools of sheepshead sometimes form around bars and other structure in the passes. At this time, anglers who find the schools of sheepshead can sometimes catch very many of the great-tasting fish. These fish are some of the hardest fish to hook in the Gulf. When they bite, most of the time they nibble and suck the bait in and spit the hook out so fast, the angler never even knows he or she has been robbed. Anglers must be very vigilant when sheepshead fishing and set the hook hard at the first sign of anything going on below. Many times, there will be no tug at all when a sheepshead bites; in fact, the line may go slack for just a second. That's when the striped robber has sucked the bait in: Set the hook! Sometimes the hook will catch, and sometimes the fish gets a free meal. When hooked, sheepshead provide a very strong and determined fight. They don't quit easily, either. While most Alabama sheepshead will weight between two and six pounds, several ten-pound and larger sheepshead are caught every year. A ten-pound sheepshead is truly a fish to be proud of: They are not easily fooled, and when hooked, they make an angler work hard to earn the catch. Anglers who have the chore of cleaning a mess of sheepshead should have a very good knife and some determination. Sheepshead are very difficult to fillet due to their unusual bone structure, but have courage! Once cleaned, sheepshead are some of the best eating around; I am very fond of Cajun-blackened sheepshead fillets.

Casting: Either spinning or casting rods and reels in medium weights—say fifteen- to twenty-pound line—will work. The rods need to be stout and also really need a fairly sensitive and responsive tip so the angler can detect the very light tapping of a feeding sheepshead. Casting distance is not nearly as crucial for sheepshead rigs as for most fish. Most sheepshead fishing is done basically straight up and down or with very short casts so that the bait will sink very close to the solid structure being fished. Fluorocarbon leaders in thirty-pound weight are a good idea when fishing for hard-pulling sheepshead near barnacle-encrusted pilings. Fluoro is more abrasion resistant than monofilament line, and also is harder to see. As far as artificial lures go, I've never caught a sheepshead on a lure, and I've never heard of anyone else catching one on a fake bait, either.

Bait fishing: To catch a sheepshead, an angler needs some small but stout hooks. I like #4 kahle hooks. These are funny-looking hooks, but they really seem to catch in sheepsheads' bony, toothy mouths better than traditional J hooks or even circle hooks.

I use only enough weight to take the bait down. Sometimes when the current is very slack or I'm fishing shallow water, I use no weight at all. In deeper water or strong current conditions—the sheepies seem to bite well in these conditions, by the way—I may go as heavy as an ounce of weight. The idea is to use the absolute minimum weight needed to help keep the sensitivity of the line at its maximum. The bait should be a medium- to small-size live shrimp. These critters will be about 2 to 3 inches long. Hook this shrimp under the horn on its head, and put it next to a piling or boulder and let it sink. Watch the line! If it twitches, set the hook. Live fiddler crabs will work well, too, and sometimes sheepies won't eat anything but fiddlers. When the fish are really actively biting, they will take dead shrimp or sometimes even chunks of squid, but this is rare. Most of the time, they want their bait live and wriggling. Now for the warning: Sheepshead have some of the biggest, sharpest, and longest fin-spines of any fish I know. Be careful when taking a sheepshead from a hook; getting finned by these fish is not fun at all. Trust me on this—I know from hard experience.

Fly fishing: Now this is an area of fishing that I feel holds some possibilities. I don't think fly anglers will ever catch many sheepshead on artificial flies; they just don't bite artificials. However, I believe that a live shrimp fished on a fly rod (sort of like a sophisticated cane pole) might work very well. I think I'll try this technique during the upcoming sheepshead season and see how it works.

Best bets: Year–round: Bon Secour River, Dog River, Fowl River, and inshore oyster reefs in Mobile Bay. In the Perdido area, try the rock jetties and underneath the high Perdido Pass Bridge.

Spotted seatrout

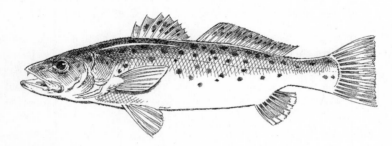

Spotted seatrout (also known as specks, speck trout, and yellow mouth) are elongated fish with a solid, very bright silver coloration with vivid black spots scattered over the sides, back, and fins. Very often, specks will have bright yellow mouths, but some also have streaks of bright blue inside their mouths, too. They have two large fanglike teeth in their upper jaws. Most spotted seatrout caught in Alabama will weigh about two pounds, but larger ones up to ten pounds are fairly common. Regardless of their size, specks are very active predatory fish that fight hard when hooked, making strong, short runs and jumping repeatedly. Also, specks can and sometimes will make surprisingly loud "thumping" noises when they are caught. They are, after all, members of the drum family, and they earn their family name. Specks are great fun to catch on top-water lures cast over oyster bars, grass beds, and other shallow structure. They love to hide in areas of current and cover and then ambush prey as it moves past them in the current. Anglers can use this feeding method and location to help pattern the fish.

Casting: A 6-foot spinning or casting rod with matching reel and fifteen-pound line will work well. Most trout are caught in fairly open water, so heavy tackle is usually not needed.

Using soft plastic tails on lead-head jigs to imitate finger mullet or shrimp is the standard procedure for catching speck trout. The soft plastic jigs are either fished alone, traditional jig style, or under a noise-making "popping cork." This cork provides weight, which makes very long casts with relatively lightweight jigs possible. The cork also makes a loud chugging sound when the line is jerked briskly, and this sound attracts feeding speck trout. This cork and jig rig is a very good setup for beginning anglers because it allows them to cast a long way, and the float helps limit bottom snags. It also catches a lot of fish.

Be careful when unhooking specks: They have a mouthful of very sharp teeth, and most of them have bright yellow-colored mouths. The neon-yellow color can be a shock to anglers who are not familiar with the fish. It's perfectly normal, however.

Bait fishing: Every year, tons of speck trout are caught on the Alabama Gulf Coast and inshore waters and bayous on live bait, mostly shrimp. Speck trout are designed to detect, catch, and eat shrimp, so it stands to reason that live shrimp should be very effective bait. A live shrimp hooked under the sharp horn on its head and cast in the vicinity of a trout will not last long. Sometimes, when a long cast is required, a live shrimp fished under a loud popping cork will bring in specks when nothing else will.

However, when size is more important than numbers, smart coastal anglers will use croakers for live bait. Croakers are small- to medium-size baitfish that are sold at most coastal live bait shops. Hooked through the lips or in the back with a fairly small treble hook and fished under a cork or free-lined in deeper water, croakers are deadly on big trout. Eight- to ten-pound trout fall victim to croakers fished this way quite often.

Don't neglect night fishing for trout. Some of the very biggest trout are caught at night by anglers fishing under lighted docks or around brightly lighted gas rigs in Mobile Bay.

Fly fishing: A fly fishery for specks in coastal Alabama is developing. In coastal areas, fly anglers can work some of the shallower reefs in Mobile Bay. Chumming is not a bad idea here to help the fish get in the mood to eat and bring them close enough to the anchored boat for a cast. Shrimp imitations and flies that resemble small mullet work well.

Best bets: To catch speck trout on a regular basis, anglers should fish any of the rivers that feed into Mobile Bay. The bay itself is full of speck trout; it's just a matter of locating the fish and getting bait in front of them. Dog River and Fowl River on the western shore are good places to start. On the eastern shore, anglers should try Weeks Bay and Bon Secour River for fast action. Most trout are caught in fairly shallow water, but they like to have deeper water close at hand in case of bright sun or very warm temperatures.

Cobia

If you can picture in your mind a shark swimming through the clear waters of the Gulf, then you have a good image of a cobia. Very often, these fine-eating, hard-pulling gamesters are confused for sharks on first glance. Both fish are similar in construction and behavior: long fish, big heads, and slow movement just below the surface until disturbed or aroused. Cobia are dark brown fish with a darker stripe down the side, and they have the white bellies of most open ocean fish. Cobia don't have the sharp stabbing or slicing teeth of many Gulf gamefish. A few cobia stay on the offshore rigs year-round, but most anglers on the Alabama Coast love cobia for their annual springtime migration along the coast from south Florida waters to off the coast of Louisiana, where they spawn and spend the summer before migrating back in the fall. In the spring, Alabama anglers spend many hours cruising the near-shore waters of the Gulf looking for these big, dark fish as they make their way to their summer grounds. At this time, cobia may be very eager to bite offerings of anglers, but they may also refuse to respond to anything cast their way. Cobia drive anglers crazy with their erratic eating behavior; perhaps this challenge is what makes some 'Bama coastal anglers find them so irresistible. When hooked, cobia make very strong runs and powerful dives with plenty of twists and turns and rolls thrown in. When finally hooked and caught, cobia are very good eating, too, and since they can get big (some fish push one hundred pounds), they provide a lot of great eating.

Casting: Some anglers choose to use medium-heavy level-wind rods and matching reels that can handle twenty-five- to thirty-pound line. The rig needs to be able to cast a long way, because cobia can get very spooky when boats approach too closely. A fifty-pound fluorocarbon leader attached to the mainline with a small, very strong swivel completes the line requirements. The same setup works for spinning gear, too. Regardless of the type of rig, the reels must absolutely have good, solid, no-stick drags because these big cobia will cause inadequate reels to fail. Cobia will hit a wide range of artificial lures, but the most commonly used artificial is a brightly colored jig of about an ounce or two with a soft plastic tail. This jig can be fished slowly or ripped through the water, and it can be cast a long way.

Bait fishing: Cobia will hit live bait such as menhaden and cigar minnows, and when on the deep reefs, they will hit just about anything. However, when on the big spring migration through the clear just-offshore waters near Alabama beaches, the best bait for cobia is often live eels. A very hot market for live eels exists here on the Alabama Gulf Coast in the spring cobia run. These snaky-looking fish are very slick and very hard to hook up for fishing. When using eels, try to put them on top of newspaper over a thick layer of ice in an ice chest. The cold keeps them alive and slows them down for easier hooking and casting. Once they hit the warm Gulf waters, they warm up and start swimming. The cobia will do the rest.

Fly fishing: Fly casting for cobia is in its infancy on the Alabama coast, but fish have been caught on the long rod when they came to a chum line in deep water. Very heavy fly gear must be used, and the reels must have plenty of backing for when the big brown fish take off on their runs. Big dark eel-looking flies would be a good bet.

Best bets: During the spring migration, anywhere along the immediate beach line from Florida to Mississippi state lines is a good place. Spring cobia fishing is more like hunting: The fish is seen before it is cast to. During the rest of the year, any of the deep reefs and gas rigs are good possibilities. Cobia just show up when and where they please.

Flounder

Now this is a funny-looking fish. Very, very flat and with a mouth full of very sharp teeth is the flounder. It is dark brown or black on top and snow white on the bottom. It lives from the inshore beaches to the bayou rivers and sloughs and offshore to the reefs. Flounder can approach ten pounds in weight, but most flounder caught in Alabama will weigh three or four pounds. Although they can bend a rod when hooked and give a fair account of themselves, flounder are not the best-fighting fish in the Gulf. So why are they so popular and eagerly sought by coastal anglers?

Flounder are ugly until they are cooked.

Flounder are delicious! They just might be my personal favorite fish to eat. Any fish recipe will work well, but grilled flounder with a nice crab-shrimp sauce is wonderful. I wish I had a big platter of flounder fillets to cook up right now! Flounder have reliable spawning runs through the Gulf passes in both spring and fall, and during the summer they are most often caught in inshore waters near structure of some kind. They will strike shrimp, but minnows are the most reliable bait. They will always be on or very near the bottom; they are bottom dwellers.

Casting: Fairly light, ten- to twelve-pound line and matching rigs will work well. Whether spinning gear or casting gear, the rod needs to be sensitive in the tip because flounder generally don't smash the bait. They like to "mouth" the offering before eating it down far enough to be hooked. Sensitive rods allow the angler to detect the bite and give the flatfish some time to complete its meal before being hooked. Most of the time, flounder will be found near docks, pilings, and oyster beds where they like to lie in ambush to capture prey swimming past. Anglers should target these areas. Flounder will hit small, one-fourth to one-half ounce jigs slowly worked along the bottom, and if the angler tips the hook with a strip of belly meat from a previously caught fish, the jig can be deadly. Again, work the jig slowly and give the flounder plenty of time to eat the bait down before setting the hook.

Bait fishing: A bucket of bull minnows, which are sold at nearly every area bait and tackle shop, are just the ticket for catching flounder. Hook the minnow through both lips from bottom to top, put a light sinker on above the hook, and cast this near a dock or old piling and let the minnow do its job. If a flounder is near, it will find the bull minnow and gobble it down. Flounder will eat shrimp, too, and sometimes very big ones prefer shrimp, but so many small fish in the same area usually beat the flatfish to the shrimp and strip it off before the flounder can eat.

Fly fishing: I don't think fly fishing accounts for very many flounder here on the Gulf Coast of Alabama. It could be done by fishing fairly large, dark-colored streamers, Clousers, and such near the bottom, but other fish such as trout and redfish would probably strike first.

Best bets: Any of the feeder streams that empty into Mobile Bay are good for flounder, but my personal favorite is Bon Secour River. I have also caught some very nice flounder in Perdido Pass on both sides.

King mackerel

The king mackerel is a very long fish, uniformly silver in color with a dark steel blue back shading to a white belly. A strong forked tail gives a great deal of power to this fish as it swims, and it never stops swimming as it must have water moving fast over its gills in order to breathe. Kings in Alabama can range in size from small "snakes" of five pounds or less to huge "smokers" of fifty pounds or more. Generally speaking, the larger fish are caught farther offshore, but every year, some very respectable king mackerel come from near-shore gas rigs and even Dixie Bar, which isn't offshore at all. A very few kings are caught from the Perdido jetty or private

Dave Powell with a good king mackerel caught on a shrimp!

piers off the beach. When the new fishing pier is completed at Gulf Shore State Park, a number of kings will be caught from it, too. At the old Gulf Shores Fishing Pier, the one that Hurricane Ivan totally destroyed, kings were fairly common during the summer months. Regardless of the size, all kings come with a full set of very sharp teeth, and they are born knowing how to use them. The angler who tries to lip a king mackerel as we do bass will only do it once. Seriously, a king mackerel can inflict some serious damage, so be careful when landing or even carrying these big fish. King mackerel are fair eating when prepared properly. I like king mackerel on the grill, wrapped in strips of bacon to help flavor the meat and make it moist, as king mackerel tends to be dry. Catching these fine gamefish is a blast; very few fish in the ocean are faster than kings, and their first run on feeling the hook is something to behold. Kings go from here to there in a very short time.

Casting: Either spinning or level-wind reels with fairly long, flexible matching rods to handle twenty- to thirty-pound line work well with kings. Since they are almost always caught in open water and they don't seek structure to tangle lines during the fight, kings can be caught from boats using pretty light line. Whether level-wind or spinning reels, the one thing that must work is the drag. Kings will stress the very best drag systems, and a substandard reel will soon lock up when the king runs, and the line will break. I've lost more nice kings to reels that weren't up to the job than for any other reason. Anglers seeking kings should use at least thirty-pound steel leader; mono leader even in very heavy weights will not last long when those teeth go to work. When fishing very clear water, the steel leader may have to be scaled down to twenty-pound, but this will mean the loss of bigger fish. Kings have very sharp eyesight, and they can be leader-shy at times. Kings will strike artificials; spoons, jigs, and billed plugs all work at times, and when the kings are schooled and really attacking baitfish, they will hit just about anything shiny.

Bait fishing: For the most consistent king mackerel catching, cigar minnows are best. Either frozen or live, rigged on "Stinger Rigs," a double hook rig very common down here on the coast, cigar minnows catch tons of kings. Cigar minnows are easily found at every bait and tackle shop on the coast. Cast the cigar minnow behind the boat and slow troll the bait. Very, very slow trolling is the game. The cigar minnow should basically sink behind the boat and just be moved very slightly by the boat's motion. For the biggest smoker kings, nothing beats a live blue runner (a very common inshore jack) hooked on the stinger rigs and allowed to swim freely behind the boat. When a king hits a blue runner of a pound or more, you can bet it's a big king, and the fight will be a struggle!

Fly fishing: Kings have been caught on the long rod while they are actively chasing schools of bait, but the fly-rod angler must be at the right place at the right time to put a big light-colored streamer in front of the kings. Again, the drag of the reel must be good because it will be tested. A good amount of backing should be loaded and ready; it will be needed, too.

Best bets: During the "king season" from April to October, just about anywhere from right off the beach to 100 miles offshore, anglers will find kings. Watch for schools of bait being attacked from below; the kings will be down there.

Red snapper

The red snapper is a fish that gives the lie to that old saying, "Beauty is only skin deep." Red snapper are gorgeous fish to see, lots of fun to catch, and just about the best thing going when cooked up right. The coast of Alabama is probably the best place in the world to catch red snapper, thanks in great part to the continued efforts

This offshore snapper was caught at the Alabama State Reefs.

of the state of Alabama and private individuals who build thousands of artificial offshore reefs each year that attract and hold these great gamefish. Red snapper are robust fish—there's nothing skinny about them—and they have mouths full of good, serviceable teeth. Their gill covers have an edge that is very sharp: Anglers need to exercise caution when handling these fish. The most common size of red snapper caught by anglers is about five to six pounds, but nearly every trip offshore at least one snapper over ten pounds comes in. Plenty of red snapper over twenty pounds are caught each year. Anglers should always be aware of the limits on red snapper; they change fairly often, and it makes a difference whether the fish are caught in state waters or federal waters offshore. There is a closed season for red snapper in Alabama; anglers must be current with the situation before heading out. There is no mistaking one of these fish when caught. They come in a wide range of red from almost orange to bright neon red. The color shades to white on the belly. Anglers should also exercise care when releasing undersize fish. Since they come from deep reefs, very often their stomachs have "blown out" of their mouths from the change of pressure. Fish to be released should be vented with a specially made needle-like tool that can be purchased at any local bait and tackle shop. This will help the released fish make it back down to deep water and safety.

Introduction

Casting: I've caught red snapper on spinning gear; in fact, my largest snapper, a seventeen-pounder, was caught on a heavy spinning rig. Most anglers choose to use pretty heavy level-wind rigs that use forty- to fifty-pound line with seventy- to eighty-pound mono leaders. Whatever the rig used, it must be capable of moving heavy, determined fish up quickly from rough territory below. Fishing for red snapper deep on the reefs is not the place for a light drag setting. Drags should be hammered down tight so that when the big fish hits, it can't pull drag and make it to the structure to break off. Penn Senator reels and matching rods are the standard for red snapper fishing in Alabama waters. Most reef fishing for snapper is pretty basic. The hook or hooks are baited, the sinker (up to nearly a pound of it in very deep water or strong current conditions) takes the bait to the bottom, the angler reels up a turn or two, and when the rod tip goes toward the water, the reel is cranked very hard indeed! Sometimes snapper can be chummed up from the deep water, and when this happens, it is very fun! When the snapper come up to see what is going on, they can be fished on considerably lighter tackle, and they really do put on a show of strong pulling and determined runs to get back deep to their home reefs. Deep jigging heavy spoons and heavy jigs tipped with squid or other live bait can be very productive for red snapper, and it is a really fun way to fish.

Bait fishing: Most red snapper in Alabama are caught on live or dead bait. Squid, chunks of cut mullet, frozen menhaden, and frozen cigar minnows all work well for deep water snapper. Live bait such as cigar minnows or pin fish work very well. For the very best and biggest snapper, the best bait is a small seabass or squirrelfish caught from the reef being fished. This little fellow is baited up on a substantial circle hook with enough weight to take it down and lowered back to the reef. It may take a few minutes, but when the big old red snapper devours the bait, the wait is worth it. Some very big red snapper are caught this way.

Fly fishing: I have heard of anglers chumming red snapper up high enough in the water column for fly anglers to cast to them and even hook them up, but it would be an unusual situation on most boats.

Best bets: Any of the state-built reefs in 100 feet or deeper water will have snapper. In fact, early in the snapper season, big reds are caught considerably shallower than 100 feet.

Spanish mackerel

The Spanish is a beautiful little fish. Elongated in shape with a strongly forked tail and a mouth full of razor sharp teeth, Spanish have intense yellow spots on their basically silver sides with steel blue backs. Their dorsal fin is deep black, which is a good field mark to help distinguish Spanish from immature king mackerel. Young kings and Spanish look very similar, but since the limits to keep are very different, anglers will want to be able to distinguish between kings and Spanish. These are flashing fast little fish—an eight-pounder is a very big Spanish—and they are a blast to catch on light gear when they are destroying schools of baitfish. Spanish leave Alabama waters in the fall when the Gulf water begins to cool, but they always return in massive schools the following spring. Unlike their much larger cousin, the king mackerel, Spanish are really very good to eat, especially when the fillets are fried in butter.

Casting: Most Alabama anglers fishing for Spanish use light tackle (ten-pound line is good) and spinning or casting rigs to match the light line. Of course, light steel leaders are required. Some folks use a short piece of heavy (fifty-pound or so) mono leader, but they get to retie lures very often as they are constantly being cut off by the teeth of the Spanish. The whole idea of fishing for Spanish is to keep a fast-moving lure in front of the school of mackerel. Since Spanish always run in large schools, the competition for baits can be intense. It is great fun to see three or four excited five-pound Spanish trying to get to your lure before their buddies can! Spanish will hit a wide range of artificial baits when they are chasing bait. Anything shiny and approximately the size of the forage fish being eaten will draw a strike from Spanish. Spoons, light-colored jigs, and even top-water plugs will gather these little speedsters in. The most productive cast lure for Spanish is the faithful old Gotcha plug. This heavy jig can be cast about a mile on light line, and it can be worked back very quickly. More than the color or size, the speed of the retrieval is crucial. Most of the time, Spanish like lures being moved at warp speed! In fact, anglers should retrieve Spanish mackerel baits as if they are trying to keep the lures away from the fish. Believe me, you can't pull the lure fast enough to get it away from a Spanish.

Bait fishing: Spanish mackerel will hit live bait, and sometimes when they are being picky, live bait is the only thing they'll take. Generally, a live cigar minnow is hooked up on a smaller version of the king mackerel stinger rig (a two-hook rig that limits short strikes and escaped fish by trailing a small treble hook on an auxiliary short leader), and the live cigar minnow is cast out as far as possible. When the Spanish see the minnow, they will circle in ever-diminishing circles around the poor minnow until one bold Spanish attacks and takes the minnow. Drags should be set fairly loose because pretty often the "Spanish" that takes the cigar minnow turns out to be a twenty-five-pound king mackerel!

Fly fishing: I have heard of fly anglers who were able to successfully use the long rod on Spanish mackerel. The main consideration for fly-rodders is not the fly—just about any medium-size, light-colored streamer will work—but the leader. Fly anglers must use at least a short length of light steel leader to keep the Spanish from taking every fly in the box!

Best bets: Spanish can and do show up everywhere along the beaches of the coast of Alabama. But I've had very good luck for the little speedsters around the Perdido Pass jetties and beaches. Spanish get thick in July about ¼ to ½ mile off the beaches all along the coast.

Map Legend

Interstate Highway	64
U.S. Highway	13
State Highway	316
County or Local Highway	70
State Boundary	ALABAMA FLORIDA
Town	○
City	◉
Capital	✪
Fishing Site	2
Overlook/Viewpoint	
Falls	
River	
Lake/Reservoir	

Coastal Region

The Gulf Coast of Alabama is not geographically a very big place. There are only about 35 miles of actual coastline, but there is so much more to the fishing scene of southernmost Alabama than this small coastline would suggest. Along with the fishing, there is so much to see and do on the coast of 'Bama. Mobile brings a wide range of activities and sports including cruise ship port of loading facilities. Small towns such as Bayou LeBattre, Lillian, and Bay Minette have unique deep-South charm that is hard to find these days. Finally, the bayous, rivers, beaches, and open Gulf itself are just spectacular places to be. There are many things that recommend the Gulf Coast of Alabama.

The Gulf Coast area offers anglers the very real chance to collect large bags of inshore gamefish such as speckled trout, redfish (my personal favorite saltwater fish), flounder, and mangrove snapper on a year-round basis. All of these fish are great fun to catch and very good fare on the table. Bag limits and size restrictions are liberal, so anglers can usually have a full day's fishing with constant catching on the inshore waters.

By the way, if eating is part of your angling activities, then you will love the Alabama Gulf Coast. Some of the world's best seafood is prepared daily in restaurants, both fancy and homey, down here. Shrimp, crabs, oysters, and fish are lovingly prepared so that no angler need faint away from hunger or undernourishment while fishing. This truly is an eater's paradise.

Coastal Alabama is a very popular vacation destination. The beaches, the surf, and the theme parks and tourist attractions make this a great place to bring the kids and family, and it's not too hard to combine family fun with some serious fishing.

The offshore fishing in Alabama is tremendous. There is a wide range of open Gulf species that are hooked and caught regularly. In the near shore waters, say up to about 8 miles offshore, king mackerel, Spanish mackerel, cobia, and jack crevalle are often brought to the boat. Go a bit farther offshore, say 10 to 30 miles off, and artificial reefs abound and so do such popular fish as red snapper, grouper, and amberjack. Go a bit farther out, say 80 to 100 miles, and you will be in the land of giants. Huge floating and anchored gas drilling rigs in the Gulf attract very big gamesters for anglers to target. These are the big tunas, big amberjack, and big billfish. There is more to catch in the Alabama Gulf waters than any single angler could catch in a lifetime of fishing.

A really good way to see all the different kinds and sizes of fish in our Gulf waters is to visit the Alabama Deep Sea Fishing Rodeo, which is held in mid-July every year from the docks at Dauphin Island. Spectators will be amazed at the fish that are brought in to be weighed and measured for prizes and research. This contest, which has been held since 1929, is a tradition for area anglers and a lot of fun for everyone involved.

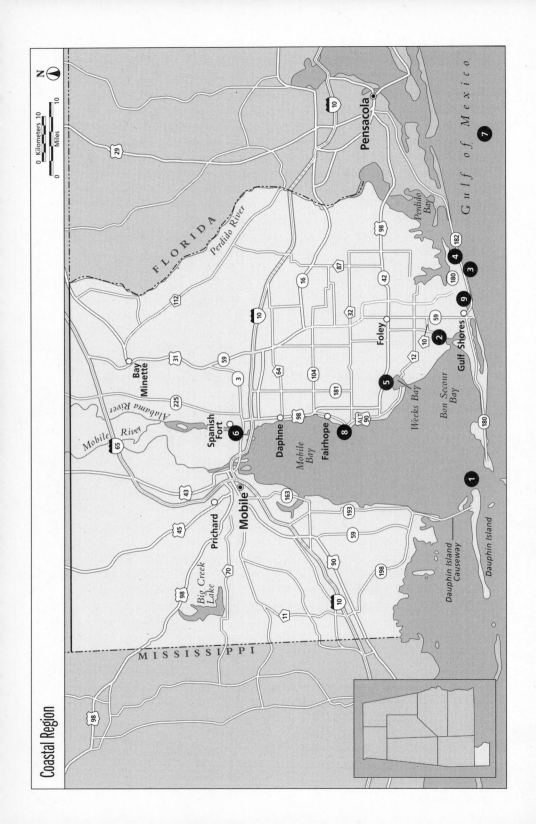

1 Dixie Bar—Mobile Bay

Key species: Redfish, jack crevalle, Spanish mackerel, king mackerel, ladyfish, flounder.

Overview: An inshore fishing spot very popular with local anglers, Dixie Bar offers the best chance to catch a really large fish without the expense of going far offshore. It is one of the best large redfish destinations in the country.

Description: Dixie Bar stretches across the mouth of Mobile Bay as it meets the Gulf of Mexico. It is a tide- and river-current-created bar of sand and silt that rises to within 5 feet of the surface and makes a tremendous ambush point for large gamefish to corner forage fish. Dixie Bar can carry very strong currents and waves. It can be hazardous to wade.

   The history of Dauphin Island, which is the west point of Dixie Bar, goes back to the earliest European exploration of the new world. Both Spanish and French explorers were well acquainted with Dauphin Island and the waters around it. Some of the very earliest European settlements in what is now the United States were built on Dauphin Island and surrounding higher points of land. During the Civil War, both Fort Morgan on the eastern shore and Fort Gaines on Dauphin Island were held by Confederate forces. It was in the Battle of Mobile Bay that Admiral David Farragut said, "Damn the torpedoes, full speed ahead!" as he urged his ships into battle. His flagship struck a mine and sank, and the wreck is still marked with a yellow buoy where it lies just north of Dixie Bar.

When the birds act like this, the big redfish are close!

Dauphin Island offers a number of interesting tourist activities, including the Exploreum, an interactive learning center; several miles of walkable beaches; and some quite good restaurants. Dauphin Island is a great place in the spring and fall migration seasons. Birders can see some very rare and interesting birds when they rest here after they arrive or when they get ready to start their cross-Gulf flights. Fort Gaines has frequent reenactments and displays, so don't be too surprised when the roar of a Civil War–era cannon rolls across the water and island.

A great deal of rental property is available, and camping is offered on the island. Two very good boat ramps are within a half mile of Dixie Bar; both are free, and parking is expansive. Weekends, of course, are much busier, so a weekday trip is less stressful.

Mobile Bay and the immediate Gulf of Mexico have several working natural gas drilling and pumping rigs that are clearly seen from Dixie Bar. These rigs present a show in themselves as work boats travel to the rigs to deliver crew and supplies. Also, a ferry runs parallel to Dixie Bar from Fort Morgan to Fort Gaines as it delivers cars across Mobile Bay. The ferry is a fun trip to let anglers and other visitors see the water, waves, and islands of the coast from the comfort of their cars. Off in the southern distance in the Gulf, the tall black brick spire of Sand Island Lighthouse can be seen on clear days. No longer working, it stands at the very entrance of Mobile Bay. The rocky shores of Sand Island are a very good fishing destination in their own right.

The fishing: Because it is a year-round fishery, just about every species of inshore saltwater gamefish can be caught on Dixie Bar at different times. However, the species that is best known and that brings national fame to Dixie Bar is redfish. These are not just any redfish, these are BIG reds. Schools of hundreds of twenty- to thirty-pound redfish form in the late fall and winter over Dixie Bar to devour the massive schools of baitfish that leave Mobile Bay and the rivers that empty into it. Anglers may encounter redfish after redfish, which are not at all hard to hook. They can be very difficult to catch if equipment and angler are not up to the chore.

A live or dead menhaden (they can be purchased either alive or frozen at any local bait shop) on a circle hook drifted with just enough weight to sink it to the bottom will not last long on Dixie Bar. The best way to locate schools of feeding redfish is to find flocks of circling and diving birds. These birds eat the same baitfish as the reds, and they seem to work together to corral the poor baitfish so they are easier to catch and eat. Cast under the birds and hang on. Although live bait is probably best, white or chartreuse-colored one-ounce jigs work very well on schooling fish, and the jigs are easier to cast long distance if the fish are spooky or are moving fast after the bait.

Since the waters of Dixie Bar are relatively open and free from obstruction, anglers are not forced to use heavy equipment. Twenty-pound line and matching spinning or casting gear is perfectly suitable, and a thirty-pound redfish on such light tackle is a fight that won't be soon forgotten.

Although the fall and winter redfish on Dixie Bar is best, the redfish never totally leave the area. Even on hot, still summer days, redfish will still be cruising Dixie Bar as they search for an easy meal. Also, in late summer, a fair run of large,

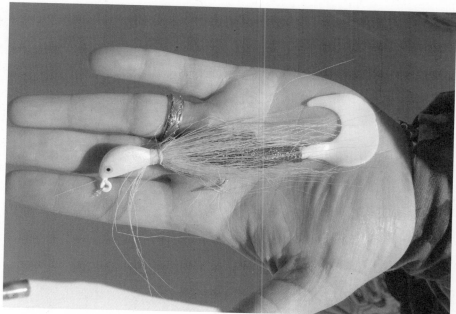

Here's a very reliable redfish lure.

mature tarpon leave the Gulf and venture across Dixie Bar into Mobile Bar. Not many tarpon are hooked, and fewer are caught, but enough of a tarpon fishery exists to make it a real possibility for any late summer angler on Dixie Bar.

DeLorme: Alabama Atlas & Gazetteer: Page 64 B4 (inset 1).

Camping: Dauphin Island Campground (109 Bienneville Avenue) is less than a mile from Dixie Bar. There are 150 sites with water and power. Clean bathhouses are on-site. Reservations are strongly urged, especially during summer tourist and winter snowbird seasons. There are many rental properties on the island.

Tips and cautions: Most of the island and the land areas around Dixie Bar are open to the public, and walking is encouraged. It is almost impossible to get lost on Dauphin Island; there is only one main east/west road, and there is only one road going on the island from the mainland. Campers should come prepared to deal with biting bugs. They aren't present at all times, but when they are there, they can be fierce.

Summers can be quite warm, and cold fronts in winter can make visitors shiver, but in general, the waters of the Gulf of Mexico and surrounding inshore waters moderate the temperature of Dauphin Island and Dixie Bar. Be aware that summer thunderstorms occur on a daily basis, and they can be quite intense; however, these summer storms don't last long.

Another caution that must be expressed is that Dixie Bar can have some very rough sea conditions from time to time. When the tide is running out strong and there is an onshore wind bringing high surf, the water right over Dixie Bar can be quite dangerous. Be careful when boating on Dixie Bar.

Directions: From Interstate 10, take exit 17A and go south on Laurendine/Highway 193 for 18 miles. The view gets very interesting the closer to the island you get. Crossing the Dauphin Island Causeway and bridge is a treat.

For more information: Alabama Marine Fisheries Division.

2 Bon Secour River

Key species: Redfish, speckled trout, flounder, sheepshead.

Overview: Bon Secour River is a slow-moving river that empties into Mobile Bay. There is light residential and commercial development on part of its banks, but even when houses and fishing companies can be seen, the atmosphere is still one of quiet and natural surroundings.

Description: The Bon Secour River runs through western Baldwin County before it empties into Mobile Bay. The funny name comes from the French, who first settled this region. "Bon Secour" means "good or safe anchorage," and apparently, this is where they brought their sailing vessels in time of bad weather. The lower reaches of the river are subject to tidal influence. Water moves out with the current

Dorothy with a very nice Bon Secour sheepshead she took on a live shrimp.

FISHING ALABAMA

on ebb tides or in against the normal river flow with flood tides. Tide flow greatly influences fishing; slack water is generally a poor time to fish. The water is never very clear in Bon Secour, but it also is almost never extremely muddy, either. The colored water supports a wide range of animals and is very rich in marine life-forms such as crabs and shrimp. There is a very active commercial fishing fleet based in the Bon Secour River and its immediate area.

There are at least two boat ramps on the lower Bon Secour. One is at Billy's Seafood, which has a $5 charge, and the other is up River Road at the dead end. This ramp is free.

In addition to the fine inshore fishing, Bon Secour gives visitors the very real possibility of seeing a wide range of wildlife. Porpoises are common and often approach closely to fishing boats. Waterfowl are quite tame, and the pelicans allow boats to approach them before they fly away. Ospreys nest in the area, and bald eagles have been seen flying over the river.

The fishing: Fishing on the Bon Secour is a year-round proposition. Summer weather may be very hot and humid, but the fishing can also be very hot. Speck trout and redfish are very often caught in the summer, fall, and spring. Flounder may show up anytime; they tend to run in bunches. However, the winter and early spring sheepshead bite can be outstanding. Sometimes in early winter, the striped buck-toothed sheepies lose all caution and bite as hard as redfish. When this happens, heavy stringers of great-tasting sheepshead are the result.

The bottom of Bon Secour River is littered thickly with hurricane-damaged dock structure and sunken boats. In some places the shoreline looks like a drowned forest with dock pilings and posts protruding form the water. These places deserve caution when boating, but they are the places to fish. Any time structure can be seen, it deserves an angler's attention. Be sure to watch your boat's depth finder: The river gets shallow very fast in places, and you don't want to run aground here.

The best technique to use when fishing this heavy sunken stuff is to get right on top of the structure and fish straight up and down, no casting. Just lower the bait and wait. If the fish are there, an angler won't have to wait long. Don't be surprised if on some occasions something big and strong takes your bait and line and keeps on going. There are some very big redfish in the Bon Secour, and they usually find a piling to break off on. Try to work the pilings from the outside edge: toward the marked navigation channel first, and then move in toward shore as needed. The reason for this technique is that fish hooked out toward the channel often run to the channel and open water. This makes them easier to catch. Fish hooked closer to the shoreline structure often run straight to the underwater pilings and other stuff in the water and break off there. Docks are very good places to cast. Fish often hold under the docks in the shadows where the water is a little cooler.

Artificial baits, usually soft-bodied jigs and scented plastic baits, work well on Bon Secour, but by far, the most reliable bait is live shrimp. Hook up a live shrimp on a small (#4) kahle hook and add a quarter-ounce sinker about a foot above the hook and that is about all that is needed. Lower this shrimp next to a piling and hold on. If there is a fish close by, he won't stay away long.

There is a bait shop, The Fresh Market, at the gas station–quick stop on Highway 59 as you turn off Highway 59 onto County Road 10 which leads to Bon Secour River. This bait shop is a very reliable source of live shrimp; I've never known them to not have good, lively shrimp on hand.

Although at least a few anglers fish the Bon Secour every day, fishing pressure is generally light. As close as it is to high traffic areas of Highway 59 and the tourist traps of Orange Beach and Gulf Shores, it is remarkable that such a quiet, low-stress place is not far away.

DeLorme: Alabama Atlas & Gazetteer: Page 64 E2 (inset 2).

Camping and lodging: No camping is close, but several motels are at Foley, only 6 or 10 miles away from the Bon Secour launch ramps.

Tips and cautions: Much of the shoreline is private; therefore, access is limited. Some landowners don't mind folks crossing, but don't assume it's all right to walk to the water just anywhere. Please ask permission first. Also, the bottom of Bon Secour is sticky, deep mud, totally unfit for wading. Don't even think about wading it. Kayaks work very well here; they are my favorite fishing craft on the Bon Secour.

Directions: From Interstate 10, take the Highway 59 exit. Go south on Highway 59 through Foley. From Highway 59, turn right at the stoplight onto County Road 10. Bon Secour River is only about 10 miles down this road. Follow the signs directing you to Billy's Seafood on Bon Secour Highway, which leads into River Road.

For more information: Alabama Marine Fisheries Division.

3 Perdido Pass—Jetty Side

Key species: Redfish, flounder, mangrove snapper, Spanish mackerel, sheepshead.

Overview: The jetty at Perdido Pass lies on the western side of the pass. It is constructed of huge boulders to help stabilize the dredged pass to the Gulf. The jetty projects perhaps a half mile into the Gulf, and it offers anglers a chance to put bait before fish that otherwise would remain out of range for beach-bound anglers.

Description: Perdido Pass jetty is a very popular shore-based fishing spot. Many locals fish the jetty often, not because it is easy but because it is productive. For a visitor, the jetty may look easy to traverse, but be aware that the large rocks are not even, the footing can be quite treacherous, and falls are not uncommon.

Parking is generous and free in the lot alongside the high Perdido Pass Bridge, but the walk from the lot to the jetties is a long one: probably ¾ of a mile or more. When fishing the jetty, take what you think you will need, but don't take anything unnecessary. The load will get heavy when you walk through soft sand on a hot day.

Be sure and take extra leaders, weights, and hooks. When fishing any rock jetty, rigging will be snagged and lost. The Perdido Pass jetty is worse than most. Carry extras of nearly everything.

FISHING ALABAMA

Redfish this size are a blast!

As in all fishing locations on the Gulf Coast, Perdido jetty puts anglers at great risk of sunburn if proper sunblock is not used. Use SPF 15 at least, and put it on thick.

Depending on the tide, the water clarity at the jetty can range from cloudy and opaque to almost crystal clear. When the water is very clear, anglers can see a wealth of underwater life swim by, and sometimes sight-fishing for certain species like redfish and sheepshead is possible. Mangrove snapper are common on the beach side of the jetty, and they love live shrimp.

The fishing: Like most coastal fishing spots, Perdido Pass jetty is greatly influenced by tide movement. Rarely is slack water a great fishing time. When the tide is either going out or moving in, fish bite better.

Fishing the jetty gives anglers a choice. On the beach side, the water tends to be more influenced by surf and wave action. It can almost be like fishing from a boat. On the Pass side, the situation is much different. Wave action is still present, but the actual current from the water moving through the Pass can make fishing this side seem very much like fishing in a strongly moving river. In general, the Pass side will require more and heavier weight to hold bait in position on the bottom.

Both artificial and live bait works on the jetty. During the summer, king mackerel are caught from the farthest end on live cigar minnows. Spanish mackerel are caught on live bait and fast-moving, shiny artificials. Redfish are present on both sides of the jetty, and during the fall and winter, sheepshead fishing can be great from both sides. Some very nice mangrove snapper can be caught from the jetties, particularly on cloudy days or early and late low-light conditions.

DeLorme: Alabama Atlas & Gazetteer: Page 64 F3 (inset 2).

Coastal Region 55

Camping: The state park at Orange Beach, Shelby State Park, has somewhat recovered from the beatings it took from Hurricanes Ivan and Katrina, and some camping is available there. A new state-owned facility is under construction at Gulf Shore State Park, and it will offer a large number of overnight choices for visitors.

Tips and cautions: Access to the jetty is somewhat limited. Anglers must walk along the seawall and not try to cross private beaches. This is not really a problem because it's the shortest path, anyway.

Directions: From Interstate 10, take Highway 59 south. Stay on Highway 59 until it stops at the beach red light. Turn left on Highway 182 and stay on this road for about 10 miles. When you see the high Perdido Pass Bridge, you're there. Park under the bridge and walk to the jetty.

For more information: Alabama Marine Fisheries Division.

4 Perdido Pass—Beach Side

Key species: Spanish mackerel, blue runners, ladyfish, bluefish, whiting, pompano.

Overview: The beach side of Perdido Pass is the eastern side, across the Pass itself from the jetty. It presents a totally different aspect to the coastal angler from the jetty. It is a much shorter and easier walk to reach the water than the jetty.

Description: The beach at Perdido Pass is easy to reach. There are a number of boardwalks across the dunes from the parking area, which make carrying gear and supplies much less of a chore than getting to the jetty. Once at the beach, visitors will be pleased with the white sand and the usually clear water of the Gulf. This is a great place to take the family to splash in the warm Gulf waters of summer while the angler catches a few inshore gamefish. Pay attention to the surf. Just because the waves are small and the Gulf is flat in the morning, that doesn't mean it will stay that way all day long. Sometimes storms far out to sea will send a heavy surf onshore, and beachgoers need to be aware of this.

During the summer tourist season, weekends can be quite busy at this beach with both locals and visitors piling up to enjoy the sun and sand. However, most weekdays are less crowded, and if a trip in early fall after school has begun can be arranged, the beach is sometimes deserted.

The fishing: Beach fishing at Perdido Pass can sometimes be very good. It gets a good tidal flow from Perdido Pass, and when the tide is moving, fish come to the beach to feed. Any bright jig or small, heavy plug that can be cast a long distance will work here. One-ounce jigs and similar-weight plugs are good. Visit any local bait and tackle shop or large discount store and ask for "pompano jigs" in the fishing section. These are light-colored jigs that have proven to be just about the most reliable artificial baits for inshore fishing. Cast as far as possible out into the Gulf and rip the bait back. You can't retrieve the bait too fast. Birds often work baitfish just off the beach, and the birds usually indicate the presence of gamefish. The most commonly caught gamefish on the beach are blue runners (locally known as hardtails), ladyfish (locally known as skipjacks), and Spanish mackerel. All of these will hit surfcaster's offerings, and all will give very good fights. A word of warning to visiting anglers who may not be familiar with saltwater fishing: Don't just reach down and lip your caught fish as you would a bass in a lake back home. Not all of the fish in the salt have teeth, but those that do have big, sharp teeth, and they will bite. I promise that if you try to lip a mackerel or a bluefish, you will never do it again! Look before you grab is a good rule down here in salt water.

Bait fishing in the surf can be very rewarding. This sort of fishing does not require heavy tackle. Normal freshwater bass gear will be fine. Twelve- to twenty-pound line is quite adequate for surf fishing. Put on an ounce sinker, tie on a #4 hook, put on a shrimp (dead or alive), and cast just outside the breaking surf. Sometimes pompano and whiting will be right in the surf, and sometimes they will be almost up on the sand. Both of these fish are great eating.

DeLorme: Alabama Atlas & Gazetteer: Page 64 F3 (inset 2).

Camping: Gulf Shores State Park is down the beach highway a few miles toward Orange Beach, and it is being rebuilt after Hurricane Ivan tore it up a few years past. Commercial camping is available in the area. Shelby State Park offers camping if it is not totally full, which it often is during the busy summer season.

Perdido Pass sheepshead love the rocks.

Tips and cautions: There are very good boardwalks that allow visitors to get to the beach without walking on the delicate dunes. Please stay on the boardwalks and don't walk on the dune vegetation. Although this information is addressed specifically to the Perdido Pass beach, it applies to any of the public access beaches on the Alabama Gulf Coast. What works here will work anywhere on the 'Bama beaches.

Perdido Pass Beach, like all Gulf Coast beaches, must be approached with just a little caution. During the summer, the sun is fierce, and folks get badly sunburned quickly without adequate sunscreen protection. Don't forget the tops of your feet and the tips of your ears! Use a high SPF sunblock, wear a hat, have a shirt with sleeves handy, and carry a beach umbrella. Keep in mind, a beach umbrella is a very good thing to have to provide some shade and cool, but it won't totally protect from sunburn. Another caution is that stingrays are common here. Very few anglers or swimmers are actually stung by stingrays, but when it happens, it is very painful, and it will bring the trip to a halt. It's hard to fish from a hospital emergency room. When wading in the surf, shuffle your feet. This keeps the angler from stepping directly on a stingray. This is particularly true when walking backward, which wade anglers do a great deal. Shuffle the feet!

Finally, watch out for purple or blue blotches of jelly on the beach. These are Portuguese man o' war jellyfish that have washed up from the Gulf. They sting and it hurts very much! Sometimes they are nonexistent, and some days they are so thick that the water is unusable. Particularly, be careful of man o'wars if your kids are with you. They seem to hurt small kids worse than adults.

Directions: From Interstate 10 take the Highway 59 exit. Go south on Highway 59 as far as it goes. When Highway 59 terminates at the beach, a stoplight will allow a left turn onto Highway 182. Head east for about 10 miles and you will cross the high Perdido Pass Bridge. Turn right off Highway 182 just past the bridge onto generous public parking areas. Restrooms and showers are at the parking area.

For more information: Alabama Marine Fisheries Division.

5 Weeks Bay

Key species: Speckled trout, redfish, flounder, white trout.

Overview: Weeks Bay is a large estuary that empties into Mobile Bay. It has light residential development on its eastern/southern shore, and almost no development on the other sides, which are largely protected. It is a large body of fairly shallow water, and it is fed by two streams, the Magnolia River and Fish River.

Description: Open water with very nicely wooded shorelines and plenty of wildlife make Weeks Bay a very nice fishing/sightseeing spot. Boaters need to be aware that the water is shallow, and that running aground is a possibility. Also, since recent heavy hurricane seasons, there is more wreckage and other obstructions in the water than in years past. Boaters should exercise caution. Both of the major tributaries, Fish River and Magnolia River, can carry boaters and anglers far up from the bay itself, and this sometimes can lead to very good fishing. It is a fun thing

Look at the teeth on this Weeks Bay speck trout.

to explore such backwaters, especially if the chance at finding some big redfish or speck trout is good.

Access is easy with boat ramps at the mouth of Weeks Bay and at ramps just off U.S. Highway 98 where it crosses Fish River. Weeks Bay presents the visitor with a wide range of natural views. Wildlife is abundant; birds particularly like this place. Porpoises are common, as are river otters. Fishing is good, particularly in the summer, fall, and late spring. Since the water is shallow, it cools fairly rapidly in the fall, and this can slow down inshore fishing somewhat. However, the fishing at Weeks Bay never completely shuts down.

The fishing: Weeks Bay has good shallow water opportunities for both speck trout and redfish, along with the occasional flounder. Live bait is probably best. Shrimp is always good, but bull minnows are especially effective on the flounder. Artificial lures work for trout and redfish, and some very good top-water action for specks occurs early and late. Redfish like soft body jigs, and if the soft plastic jig body is one of the newer scented brands, it is even better. Fairly often, big jack crevalle come into Weeks Bay from Mobile Bay to feed on the massive schools of baitfish that occupy Weeks Bay. If you hook into one of these big bad boys, you are in for a thrill. They pull very hard, and they don't quit quickly. There is a good summer-fall run of redfish at the very bottom of the bay where it empties into Mobile Bay. The water here at "Big Mouth," as it is locally known, drops off to 40 feet deep or more, and it can provide hot fishing when the reds come in to feed on shrimp.

Coastal Region

DeLorme: Alabama Atlas & Gazetteer: Page 63 H6.

Camping: A private campground is just past the US 98 crossing. Fish River runs beside the campground, and dockage and ramps are on-site.

Tips and cautions: Weeks Bay is a somewhat protected area. Folks live here, but they don't seem determined to spoil the bay with overdevelopment. This is a very nice place to take the family for a boat ride and to explore some of the out-of-the-way places, all the time being in perfect safety. Since Weeks Bay is protected on practically all sides from strong wave action, there is almost never a problem with rough seas.

Access is easy with ramps at both ends of the bay, and except for the before mentioned underwater hazards of shallow water and some storm wreckage, Weeks Bay is a very safe place to fish.

Directions: From Interstate 10 turn onto Highway 59. Go south on Highway 59 until the main stoplight in Foley. Turn right onto US 98. It will cross Fish River/Weeks Bay in about 12 miles.

For more information: Weeks Bay National Estuarine Research Reserve; Alabama Marine Fisheries Division.

6 Mobile-Tensaw Delta

Key species: Largemouth bass, catfish, assorted sunfish, crappie; saltwater species at different times and conditions.

Overview: Stretching north of Interstate 10 for about 15 miles, the Mobile-Tensaw Delta is protected from development, and the wild things that live there—bears, bobcats, alligators in great abundance, deer, wild hogs, and even some panthers—wander free and make their livings in the great swamp. Even manatees are seen here on occasion. The Delta is a birdwatcher's paradise, especially in the spring and fall when migratory birds mass here before their flight across the Gulf. Swallowtail and Mississippi kites and bald eagles live here.

Description: This is a place like no other. The Mobile-Tensaw Delta is big, wild, and full of things that can't be seen in many other places. It is also within visual distance of the second largest city in Alabama. The Mobile Delta is a place of contradictions.

Many people use the Delta for recreation and as a way to make a living, and it is still very likely that when you go fishing here, you won't see anyone else while you are on the water.

Big rivers, smaller bayous, shallow flats, forested bottomland that floods periodically, ox-bow lakes full of fish—the Mobile-Tensaw Delta almost defies description. An angler can fish the Delta in a wide range of ways, but almost all involve a boat. Some bankside fishing is possible, and even though a few ramps and parks offer shore fishing, the great majority of fishing here is boat based.

The water here is cloudy, sometimes quite muddy, and it is full of life. These waters serve as a vast nursery for many species of fish and other waterlife such as

Mobile Delta has many swamps and backwaters that are great to explore by kayak.

shrimp, crabs, and other species. The river currents are slow, but they cannot be underestimated. In times of flood, both the Tensaw and Mobile Rivers can roll right along. Most of the time, the river currents are quite manageable.

Access to the Delta is limited, but anglers can put in at the Causeway, and at several ramps and launch areas up both sides of the Delta. A very important point to keep in mind when fishing the Mobile-Tensaw Delta is that you will want to wind up back where you started. A GPS system is a nice thing to have on a boat, but it is almost a necessity on the Delta. Once you are out of sight of the ramp, it is very easy to get very lost. The creeks, bayous, and other waterways start to look alike, and the Delta is covered with very tall vegetation of all kinds, which block any open, orienting view. Each year, folks go into the Delta and have to be rescued. Every indication is that a night spent lost in the dark on the Mobile-Tensaw Delta is a very long, dark, mosquito-ridden night indeed.

When fishing the Delta, be careful, and watch the tide! Being connected to the Gulf and massive Mobile Bay, the Delta is somewhat subject to tide influence, and if your boat runs out of water, you CANNOT get out and push. The bottom in the Delta is composed of very soft, sticky, apparently bottomless mud, and if you try to get out and push a stuck boat, you will be stuck, too. Don't ask me how I know this. Take my word for it.

The fishing: Fishing in the Delta is almost indescribable. North of the Causeway, freshwater fish live in profusion. By the way, remember that north of I-10, you must have a freshwater license. South of I-10, it's a saltwater license you need. Largemouth bass are thick; they don't seem to get as big as some of the bass in the larger reservoirs up north, but there are lots of them, and five- to seven-pound fish are fairly common. They respond to normal bass technique and baits. Fifteen- to twenty-pound spinning or level-wind gear will work fine, and the Delta bass like spinner baits, plastic baits of all kinds, and stick-type top-waters early and late. Several major bass tournaments are held each year in the Delta. Some very good bass are taken from offshoots of the main rivers. If an angler has a shallow draft boat (most bass boats will work), there are some excellent side waters that hold very good bass. Byrnes Lake off the Tensaw River is a good example. Anglers can cast plastic baits up into underwater cover and hook up with some dandy bass.

Catfish are quite common and quite large in the two major rivers and in the larger bayous. Limb lines and jugs are used for catfish, as well as handheld gear. Large bait (shad, bream, and shrimp) catch the catfish. Anglers will want to use multiple rods and reels to help find the depth and bait preference of the cats. Most days, the catfish are willing to bite on nearly anything.

In the spring, major tributaries such as Bay Minette Creek have a good run of crappie, and bream also are thick at this time. As the season moves on, the panfish tend to find deeper water and spend their time there. During the winter, some very big bream in large concentrations can be found in the major feeder creeks in deeper pockets. A good fish finder is very valuable at this time to help identify the fish and their location.

Of course, the most remarkable thing about fishing in the Mobile-Tensaw Delta is the wide range of fish that are caught there. It is not only possible but very probable that an angler there will catch a largemouth bass on one cast, and on the very next cast into the same pocket with the same bait, he or she will catch a salt-water species such as a redfish or a speckled trout or a flounder. This is particularly the case with anglers who use soft plastic jigs and spinner baits. The fish don't observe human boundaries, and they move from one ecosystem to another. Sharks are known to swim far up the two major rivers.

DeLorme: Alabama Atlas & Gazetteer: Page 62 D5, C5, B5.

Camping: Several of the fish camps—the local name for private river-access points—up the Tensaw River offer camping as well as boat launch facilities. A very nice state park, Meaher Park, on the Causeway, is very well identified and easy to find, and it gives visitors a boardwalk to view the Delta from slightly above water level. A boat ramp is at the park. There is camping at Meaher Park.

Tips and cautions: Ramps are open on the Causeway, and there is at least one good bait shop on the Causeway that offers boat launching as well as live shrimp. On the eastern shore of the Delta, several fish camps and landings offer anglers easy access. Bay Minette Creek, Cloverleaf Camp, Byrnes Lake, Cliff's Landing, and Hurricane Landing all put anglers on the Tensaw River.

Don't think that the Delta is totally benign. The one creature you can count on seeing here is Mr. Gator. There are thousands of alligators in the Delta, and they range from little hatchlings of 8 inches long to 15-footers that are at the top of the food chain.

Now here's the warning: Alligators don't want you, but they do want your dog. There are no reports of alligators attacking people, but every year, tourists and residents alike lose dogs to 'gators. I would not take a dog with me fishing in the Delta.

Mosquitoes are residents of the swamps, and they will bite. A good insect repellent is in order.

Directions: From I 10, turn on the U.S. Highway 98 exit at Spanish Fort. Go north about a mile on US 98 until it intersects with Highway 90. Turn left (west) and this four-lane road will lead directly to the Causeway and access to the Delta.

For more information: Alabama Marine Fisheries Division; Mobile-Tensaw Wildlife Management Area.

Good Eats

It is remarkable, but anglers fishing the wilds of the Mobile-Tensaw Delta are very close to some excellent eating places. On the Causeway are several restaurants, and they are all very good—really. You just can't go wrong out here. I've eaten at all of them. However, for the very BEST Cajun steamed crawfish I've ever found, try R&R Seafood. Those mudbugs are great!

7 Alabama State Reefs

Key species: Red snapper, grouper, triggerfish, king mackerel.

Overview: We can't leave coastal Alabama without mentioning the world-class offshore fishing in the Gulf. Alabama currently has the largest artificial reef deployment program in the world, and the fishing in Alabama's portion of the Gulf is far and away much improved because of the reef program.

Description: It's a fact that the natural bottom of the Gulf off Alabama's shores is very uninteresting. It's flat and there is no structure. Where there is no structure, there are no fish. Ever since the early 1950s, anglers and state government have worked together to put car bodies, old ships, road demolition material, Army tanks, and other stuff on the bottom. The result of this is Alabama's world-class reef fishing. Even though Alabama has a tiny Gulf coastline, the red snapper fishery is just about the best in the world. The natural gas drilling rigs that dot the Alabama coast and offshore waters provide excellent fish-attracting structure.

Both Dauphin Island and Orange Beach offer high-class facilities for visiting anglers to charter a big-game fishing trip to the reefs, or if the angler is lucky enough to have a boat capable of the open-water trip, ramps and docks are available at both places.

Fishing the Alabama State Reefs is an adventure. Every trip is different. Some days the Gulf is flat calm with barely a chop, and some days the Gulf is much too rough to even consider venturing out for fishing. Each day requires judgment and discretion. Anglers should check with local guides, tackle shops, and fishing reports to determine conditions, tide schedules, and exactly what bait to use.

Attention to weather, not just present conditions but also to potential development, is crucial for a safe trip. Obviously, any boat being taken offshore must be in good working order, and all requirements for safe operation must be met. Communication gear, both VHF and cell phone, is very important in case of trouble. NOAA radio weather is helpful for offshore anglers.

This gag grouper came from inshore structure.

FISHING ALABAMA

The offshore reefs and gas rigs are places for heavy saltwater gear and rigging. Gear capable of handling heavy, strong fish and moving these fish up off deep-water reefs is necessary. Although many anglers use what is essentially freshwater bass gear successfully while fishing in the Gulf, when the big one strikes and heads off fast, twenty-pound line just won't slow him down much.

The fishing: Most anglers going out to the Alabama State Reefs use live bait. Cigar minnows, menhaden, or smaller reef fish caught while on the reef will work well. Most reef anglers use heavy level-wind rigs capable of handling seventy-five-pound line and four- to ten-ounce sinkers.

This tackle may seem like overkill, but there are lots of fish on the reefs that require this sort of tackle. For instance, on a recent trip I took offshore, my buddies on the boat with me (Dave Powell, Nate Butler, and my son Rob) and I were catching king mackerel on one of the Alabama State Reefs; it was an old Liberty ship that had been sunk in the '60s. The kings were biting hot, and we were having a blast with the fifteen- to twenty-pounders. One of the other guys had a king hooked and on the way to the boat when his line suddenly went slack. All of a sudden there was no king, no leader, no hook. We saw a shadow deep in the clear water below us, and we realized that we had a visitor. For the next hour, just about every other king mackerel we hooked became a snack for the 9-foot-long, 300- to 400-pound hammerhead shark that cruised below us. Our standard king mackerel rigs—twenty-five-pound spinning rods and line—didn't even get that big boy's attention when he took our fish. While fishing offshore, anglers may see nearly anything that swims in the Gulf.

While fishing a reef, an angler can expect to catch red snapper, grouper, and triggerfish on a consistent basis. Live bait dropped to the structure will soon be gobbled up, and the angler had best get the fish coming up quickly; otherwise, the fish will be back down in the reef, and the angler will be hung up and the fish will be lost.

The Alabama State Reefs attract a wide range of Gulf species. While on another trip to the state reefs, I had a lighter spinning rig ready when a dolphinfish flashed past our boat. I made a cast, the dolphin took, and a bit later I had a gorgeous cow dolphin in the box. Just about anything out there can show up at nearly any time.

In short, the state reefs are grand places to go if the angler has a craft big enough and equipped to make the trip.

As far as actually finding the reefs, Alabama's Marine Resources Division of the Department of Conservation makes all state reef locations available to anglers on the Outdoors Alabama Web site (see Appendix). Latitude and longitude numbers are given for all deployment areas.

Probably the easiest way to make the trip to the state reefs is to either charter a boat out of Dauphin Island or Orange Beach. There are several listings on the Internet that will direct anglers to fishing boats. Many anglers who don't want to spend quite as much money (private charters can get pretty high-dollar) go out on party boats. For about $100 per person, anglers can get offshore and into some very good fishing. Again, these boats can be found either at Dauphin Island marinas or marinas at Orange Beach.

For anglers using their boats, basically it comes down to two options. Launch at the ramps at the eastern end of Dauphin Island and motor out over Dixie Bar past Sand Island Lighthouse to the deployment zones, or put in at either Cotton Bayou Ramps at Orange Beach or Boggy Bayou ramps, also at Orange Beach. There are other ramps, but these ramps are well-maintained, easy to access, and best of all, free.

Check with local area tackle stores to get up-to-the-minute advice on what's biting, where, and on what. Also, it won't hurt to buy some fresh bait at the shop.

DeLorme: Alabama Atlas & Gazetteer: Page 64 B3, B4 (inset 1); page 64 E-4 (inset 2).

Camping: On Dauphin Island, a campground is just across from the Billy Goat Hole ramps. At Orange Beach, Gulf State Park is close. At both places, rental property of all levels and costs are available for visitors.

Directions: For Dauphin Island: From Interstate 10 take the exit for Highway 193 and follow it all the way south; it will lead directly to Dauphin Island. The fishing marina is on the left as you come off the bridge.

For Orange Beach: From I-10, take the Highway 59 exit at Loxley and go south until the highway dead-ends at the beach stoplight. Turn left on Highway 182 and go on for about 10 miles. Perdido Pass and the largest group of charter boats will be there.

For more information: Alabama Marine Fisheries Division; U.S. Army Corps of Engineers.

8 Fairhope Pier

Key species: White trout, speckled trout, flounder, redfish, various sharks.

Overview: Fairhope Pier gives anglers a chance to fish for big fish and yet never have to go aboard a boat or get too far from the shelter of a car in case the weather gets bad. Located on Mobile Bay's eastern shore where the beautiful old town of Fairhope meets the water, Fairhope Pier gives anglers a good shot at hot fishing, cool breezes, and some of the best sunsets to be found anywhere. In addition to the convenience of the pier for shore anglers, there is a good boat ramp just north of the pier, within 100 yards.

Description: Badly damaged by Hurricane Katrina, the Fairhope Pier has been rebuilt to provide shorebound anglers very good easy access to saltwater fishing. Although the pier gets many pedestrian visitors who put in their exercise miles by walking the decks during the daytime hours, after dark the crowds thin out, the lights come on, and the fish generally bite. This is a very well-maintained and clean place to bring the family. Access is very good for handicapped anglers, with wheelchair ramps from the parking area. The pier gives anglers great views of sailboats, water birds, and other life in the water. There are covered pavilions on the pier for sun protection. There is even a restaurant on the pier and marina facilities at the pier. There is no charge to walk or fish on the pier.

The fishing: The fishing, especially at night, is surprisingly good. Although most

Fairhope Pier is a great place to spend a beautiful afternoon.

anglers would not expect fishing to be good in such a "civilized" place, after the sun goes down and the Jet Skis go to bed, fish really come alive around the pier. The most commonly caught fish are white trout. They aren't big, usually a pound to two pounds, but they fight well, and they are quite good fried up. All of the trout (white, silver, or speckled) are much better when prepared absolutely fresh. They are not good fish at all when frozen; they turn mushy. Speckled trout are less common, but they do show up. Pieces of dead shrimp work best for white trout. Don't let them run with the bait long; they are masters at bait stealing.

Flounder are very often taken near the pilings of the pier, and they are the best eating in the Gulf. Flounder take live shrimp or bull minnows sent to the bottom with a slip sinker of about one ounce weight.

Very rarely will a night go by without someone hooking a shark (sometimes a big one); big redfish cruise through, and they provide a very good battle. Both of these hard pullers will respond to cut bait or even live shrimp. If you are serious about hooking a shark, invest in steel leader and big circle hooks. Monofilament, no matter what test, will not hold a shark for long.

Finally, it doesn't happen often, but rarely in the late summer months, a tarpon will visit the pier and be hooked. They don't stay hooked long because they are always very large, mature fish, but they are a thrill to angler and onlookers alike.

Bait to be used on the Fairhope Pier is simple. Shrimp, either live or fresh frozen, is the ticket. Use just enough weight to take the shrimp to the bottom, and get comfortable. The bite usually doesn't take long.

Coastal Region

DeLorme: Alabama Atlas & Gazetteer: Page 62 E5.

Camping and lodging: No camping is nearby, but a number of private bed-and-breakfasts and other rental property are within walking distance of the pier.

Tips and cautions: The town of Fairhope is in walking distance to the pier, and for nonfishing family members, it offers a wide range of arts, crafts, shopping, and eating choices. It's a nice place.

Directions: From Interstate 10, take Alternate U.S. Highway 98 south into Fairhope itself. Direction signs provided by the city will guide the motorist to the park and pier area.

For more information: Alabama Marine Fisheries Division; City of Fairhope.

9 Lake Shelby—Gulf State Park

Key species: Largemouth bass, catfish, bream, occasional redfish.

Overview: Lake Shelby is a strange place in a certain way. Even though it's on a Gulf of Mexico beach, it is in fact a freshwater lake. The fishing in Lake Shelby really bears no resemblance to that in the Gulf. The lake's white sandy beaches contrast with its dark but clear water. There are good boat ramps for easy access to the lake, and much of the shoreline is cleared for easy bank fishing by park visitors.

Bream grow big in Lake Shelby.

FISHING ALABAMA

Description: Even though Lake Shelby is very close to a popular tourist area, and hundreds of visitors camp in the campgrounds on its shores, it is not a completely civilized lake. Much of the shoreline is still heavily brushed, and many forms of wildlife still live on or in the lake. Lake Shelby is good place to see waterfowl of many kinds, including ospreys and other hawks. There are alligators in the lake, so very small children and pets must be watched. Also, the Gulf beaches are an easy walk from the lake and campgrounds, so an angler can easily fish Lake Shelby in the morning for bass and other fish, and then catch saltwater gamesters such as mackerel, jacks, and ladyfish later in the day. Anglers must be aware of the lake's alligators; some are quite bold and will approach anglers for a handout. Don't feed them!

The lake is very easily accessed by car; it's just off the busy beach road in southernmost Alabama, and it gives folks a good place to take a break from the sometimes hectic traffic during busy tourist season. Swimming and pleasure boating are allowed here. There are good restrooms and showers here as well as gorgeous picnic areas. Lake Shelby is not just a "summer" destination. Highly recommended is the "snowbird" season of winter. Many northern residents are happy to escape the cold and snow of the Midwest and northern states to come down here to enjoy the springlike winter conditions. Fish still bite in winter, too.

The fishing: Fishing in Lake Shelby can be very good, especially if the angler can get away from the more heavily used areas around the campground and pavilions.

Bass bite well on deep-running crankbaits, and bright soft plastic tube lures do well, too. Early in the morning or late in the afternoon are good times for top-water lures. Live bait such as big minnows work on bass, and so do live shrimp. Live shrimp can be found in nearly every local live-bait shop, and the bass love them as much as everything else does. Hook up the shrimp under the horn on its head, attach a bobber about 3 feet above the hook, and cast this near some deeper water or shoreline structure. Bass love it! If an angler has a small boat to launch at the ramps and then head to the far side away from the park area, the fish seem to bite better.

Catfish respond well to shrimp fished on the bottom. They don't seem to get as big as those caught in area rivers, but even two-pound catfish fry up just fine.

Bream seem to be everywhere, but anglers may have to cull through several small ones to make a mess of fish to fry. This is a good place to bring a light rod and reel, a can of worms, and a kid to learn about fishing. The little bream are very agreeable, and kids love it. A word of caution: I have seen alligators in Lake Shelby who thought those red-and-white bobbers were lots of fun to bite and crush. Keep an eye on the kids and explain to them what is going on; they will probably find it very amusing.

Also, anglers should not be surprised if something very big and strong takes a bait here. There are a few big redfish that have either been released into the lake or got here from heavy storm water from the Gulf. If one of these bad boys takes your bait, it will be a struggle.

DeLorme: *Alabama Atlas & Gazetteer:* Page 64 F3 (inset 2).

Camping: Lots of camping options are very close. There are primitive camping, RV sites, and cottages. During the heavy tourist season of summer, the camp can fill up, so early reservations for camping are needed. The Gulf State Park campground is located at 22050 Campground Road, Gulf Shores, AL 36542; (251) 948-6353.

Tips and cautions: The Lake Shelby area took a very hard hit from Hurricane Ivan a few years back. Reconstruction of the main park facilities on the beach is ongoing, and for quite a while, the park's campground area was taken over by FEMA in order to give storm evacuees a place to live. Progress is good on the park rebuilding, and Lake Shelby itself is back open for business.

Directions: From Interstate 10, take Highway 59 south until it intersects the beach road, Highway 182, at Gulf Shores. Go left on Highway 182 for about 7 miles. Lake Shelby and the park will be on the left at the stoplight.

For more information: Alabama Wildlife and Freshwater Fisheries Division; Alabama Gulf State Park.

Good Eats

There are LOTS of great places to eat in this area, but one of my favorites is the Shrimp Steamer, just off Highway 59 behind the giant shark tourist shop. Very good food!

Southwest Region

The southwestern region of Alabama requires anglers to exert a little more energy than some places. The rivers and streams in this area are big, and they can be difficult to master. However, once an angler learns the ropes and the ways of each lake and river here, some very impressive catches of gamefish can be made.

As with all dams, the big dams on the rivers in southwestern Alabama demand attention from anglers because water conditions can change quickly, especially when the dam releases water to generate electricity. An angler anchored below a dam must make sure that the boat is handling the increased flow adequately. However, when the water flows are strong, the fish tend to really bite well, too.

In short, the southwestern region of Alabama is a fine place to come for a fishing trip or a fishing vacation; there are many places to wet a line, and good fish are just waiting to provide a battle.

10 Claiborne Lake

Key species: Largemouth bass, catfish, crappie, various bream, striped bass.

Overview: Claiborne Lake is another of the string of Alabama River lakes that are created by navigation dams. It is one of the less developed lakes on the Alabama River chain, and folks who are looking for a place to get away from crowds on the water might want to investigate this lake.

Description: Claiborne Lake stretches for 244 river miles, and more than thirty creeks and other feeder streams join at various points along the lake's run. Seen on a map, Claiborne Lake looks like a river; there are no wide-open stretches of water. Anglers here must also be aware that the lake is very subject to upstream rainfall, or the lack of it. As of this writing, Alabama is in a years-long drought, and water levels everywhere are low. This is particularly true of the Alabama River lakes, including Claiborne, so anglers need to exercise even more caution when navigating the lake. Obstructions that are normally well under the surface are now exposed.

There are good access points; it's not a total wilderness area, but there are just not many lakeside homes and other buildings to be seen. Because at this point the Alabama River is down out of the hills, the flow is slower and the water is more stained in color, but it is still a very nice place to visit and fish.

The fishing: Fishing at Claiborne is primarily a spring and fall situation. Fish are still caught in summer and winter, but most anglers focus their effort during the hot spring run of fish below the Claiborne dam. Bass anglers work spawning fish in the backwater and side lakes. In particular, bass are caught in Sills Creek area and in Stump Lake, a flooded woodland that has rotted away until only the underwater

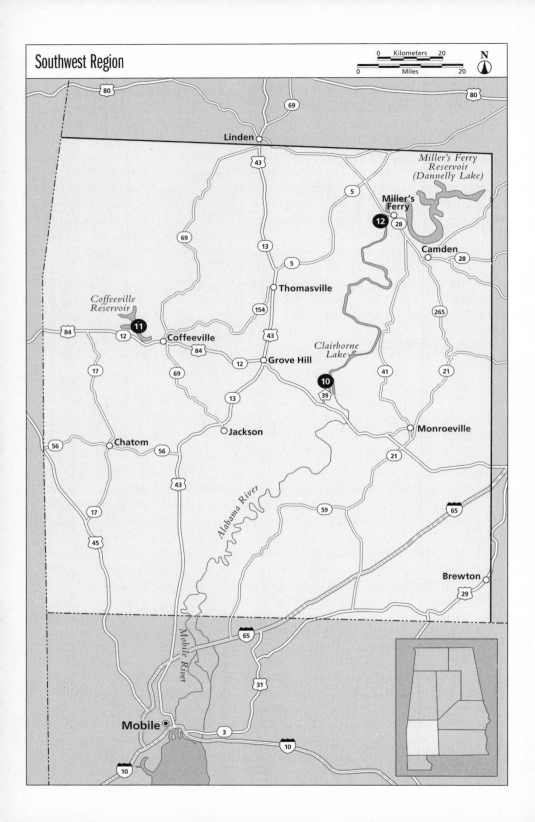

Southwest Region

Backwaters of all big rivers are good early spring locations.

structure remains. Soft plastics, particularly large dark-colored worms, spinner baits, and top-water baits and buzz baits, can be good for largemouth.

Catfish are probably the most popular target of anglers in Claiborne Lake, and the entire Alabama River chain for that matter. Anglers seeking catfish should look for deeper pockets with current, and fish these holes carefully starting at the up-current end and working down toward the end of the pocket. Live baits, especially chicken gizzards, frozen shrimp, and crawfish, are good. Commercially prepared catfish baits will work as well. Some very big catfish swim here, so anglers should not come undergunned. Fifty-pound line and gear is not too heavy. Anglers should pay attention to the current conditions. If the dam stops pumping water, it may be time to head home. The water needs to be moving with a decided current in order for the bigger catfish to go on the prowl.

In the spring, bank anglers have a party below Claiborne Dam when striper and hybrids run upstream to spawn. Boat anglers have good success, of course, but shore-bound anglers can do just as well on the big silver battlers by presenting live shad and shad look-alike artificial lures. There is a pretty big drop from the fishing platform to the water, and, of course, a few fish are lost in the transfer from water below to walkway above, but there are usually plenty to make up for the loss.

DeLorme: Alabama Atlas & Gazetteer: Page 48 H10.

Camping: An excellent option is found at Isaac Creek Campground, which offers sixty sites with full hookups and facilities. This campground puts anglers right on the water with many sites, and it is never overcrowded and noisy. Campers can often see 'gators swimming in the creek behind their campsites. Good ramps are at Davis Ferry off County Road 17. Below the dam, the ramps just off U.S. Highway 84 are also good.

Tips and cautions: Anglers have access to a well-stocked bait and tackle shop near the dam site. This is a good place to obtain live bait.

Directions: From Grove Hill, take US 84 east to County Road 39. Follow CR 39 north. This will take the angler to the dam site.

For more information: U.S. Army Corps of Engineers; Alabama Wildlife and Freshwater Fisheries Division.

11 Coffeeville Reservoir

Key species: Bass, crappie, bream, catfish, hybrid striped bass, striped bass.

Overview: Coffeeville Reservoir is on the Tombigbee River. It is an impounded lake of nearly 9,000 acres that runs from near Coffeeville 97 miles to Demopolis.

Description: This is a large, dammed river lake, and it is used for commercial navigation in addition to its recreational uses. There are a number of feeder river and creek arms that provide reliable fishing. In fact, the feeder streams are often the preferable places to fish, especially during the spring.

There are several nearby towns that can provide supplies, equipment, services, and places to stay. There is a campground close to the dam.

The fishing: Largemouth bass fishing is good in the feeder creeks and rivers off the main lake body. Crankbaits and plastic baits are very effective. As far as all of the Tombigbee River Lakes go, Coffeeville Reservoir has a good population of shad as forage for the bass, and accordingly, anglers should use this to their advantage. Fairly large light-colored crankbaits worked along drop-off and river and creek channels can be very effective on bass in the spring. Later in the summer, good results come from jig and pig combos fished around deeper logjams and other structure. If an angler can locate a deep log, say 12 to 15 feet deep, with some current from the main lake body or a feeder creek working either against the log or down the length of the log, this can be a great setup for fast bass action. Winter fishing for bass can be good, especially in deeper feeder creeks that receive a little warm rain run-off.

Crappie are caught up the creeks also, but they prefer live minnow or small tube-type jigs. Anglers may have to go pretty far up some of the larger feeders to get to the crappie's preferred spawning depths, but they will be there in about 3 feet of water, usually around some sort of wooden structure. Brush piles, fallen limbs, and especially standing timber are all good places to start a search for springtime spawning crappie. Try a small jig (one-eighth ounce is good) suspended under a

A calm morning at Coffeeville, but big bass are waiting.

small bobber. Cast it into likely areas and just let it sit. Often, the action of the little bobber on the waves is enough to move the tiny jig and catch the spooky crappie's attention. A little live minnow added to the jig is just icing on the cake. If a crappie doesn't hit that setup, there just aren't any crappie there and you can move on.

In the tailwaters of the dam, catfish are targeted by using whole shad drifted with the current. This is heavy tackle fishing, for sure. Anglers for these big tailrace cats should use fifty-pound or heavier line, and enough weight to take the bait to the bottom. Depending on the water moving through the dam, this may be a lot of weight. Each day is different, so be prepared to experiment. The rule is just enough weight to get to the bottom, but no more. Excess weight will just lead to hang-ups and lost tackle; that will happen enough at the best of times! Some very large catfish are caught below Coffeeville Dam.

DeLorme: Alabama Atlas & Gazetteer: Page 48 E4.

Camping: Service Campground is located just up from the dam.

Tips and cautions: Several points of access are available on the lake. In addition to the lake itself, Choctaw National Wildlife Refuge is on the lower reaches of the lake.

Anglers should be aware of larger vessel traffic and make sure to give plenty of room to commercial craft.

Southwest Region

Directions: From Grove Hill take U.S. Highway 84 west to Coffeeville. Continue west on US 84; the Coffeeville Lake Project will be on the right.

For more information: U.S. Army Corps of Engineers; Alabama Wildlife and Freshwater Fisheries Division; Demopolis Chamber of Commerce.

12 Miller's Ferry Reservoir (Bill Dannelly Lake)

Key species: Largemouth bass, crappie, catfish, striped bass.

Overview: Created in 1969, Miller's Ferry is a large 17,200-acre reservoir on the Alabama River. It has 516 miles of shoreline. There is much structure present to hold fish.

Description: Miller's Ferry is a large, dammed-river reservoir that provides high-quality angling to southwest Alabama. There are large areas of flooded timber. It is a superior large-bass lake, with the average fish running about three pounds. It is a fertile lake, which contributes to the high forage fish population. Anglers should be conscious of larger vessel traffic that also uses the lake.

The fishing: Plastic baits are always good for largemouth bass, as are spinner baits. Fairly large sizes and light colors are best. It may take a big, noisy bait to catch a large bass's attention. Try working large, dark-colored plastic worms slowly near

Big rivers and big dams provide great fishing.

underwater structure such as logs and brush piles. Since there is a large shad population in the lake, crankbaits and jerk baits in shad patterns are good. Try walking a Zara Spook on dark, overcast days.

Creeks off the main lake body are very good locations to find heavy concentrations of crappie in the spring, but the crappie fishing is quite good during the winter, also.

Most anglers catch crappie on live minnows. It may take some work to finally locate good numbers of crappie, but when they are found, they tend to come in fast.

Catfishing in the tailrace waters below the dam can be excellent, with several large (thirty pounds or more) channel and blue catfish caught annually. Some very big catfish are chased and caught by specialists who fish the big Alabama River lakes just to connect with big cats. Live shad are great baits, but dead shad and other prepared catfish baits will work, too. Below the dams are great places to catch big cats; they pile up in the strong water to eat shad and other baitfish, which are taken through the turbines.

During their spring run, hybrid stripers and stripers congregate in the dam tailwaters, also. Stripers can be caught during the summer in the main body of the lake around cool water springs and creeks.

DeLorme: Alabama Atlas & Gazetteer: Page 43 H7.

Camping: Try the Corps of Engineers public-use areas at East Bank, Six Mile, and Chilatchee Creek. Camping is also available at Roland Cooper State Park.

Tips and cautions: Camden is close at hand and offers fishing tackle, lodging, and restaurants. Several other activities such as golf are nearby. Very good public ramps are found at Cobbs Landing below the dam and above the dam at L & L Marina, Gees Bend, and Cooper State Park. Also upstream is Bogue Chitto Creek Landing.

Directions: From Camden, go 12 miles northwest on Highway 28. Turn right before Lee Long Bridge.

For more information: U.S. Army Corps of Engineers; Alabama Wildlife and Freshwater Fisheries Division; Wilcox Area Chamber of Commerce. Hours of power generation for both Jones Bluff and Miller's Ferry can be obtained at (334) 682-4655.

Southeast Region

For some reason, when I visit or think about the southeastern region of Alabama, I feel more "Southern" than the rest of the state. It's not logical, I know, but this part of Alabama and its many fishing spots just seem to be a little slower-paced, a little less developed, and more in tune with "the way things used to be."

Here anglers will find one of the most famous largemouth bass fishing lakes in the world. Bass anglers everywhere have heard of Lake Eufaula and its fabulous bass fishing. However, there are other very good fishing sites here, too. Some good lakes and reservoirs lie in this part of the state, but it is the rivers that gather a lot of attention here.

Anglers who, like myself, enjoy floating down a stream, fishing, and just observing the natural world as it rolls by with the movement of the current will like this part of Alabama. There are some of the last free-flowing streams in the state here, and even the streams that are dammed quickly lose the "tamed" look of many dammed streams and very soon revert back to their natural state. There are some big old catfish to be caught in the rivers of southeastern Alabama.

13 Choctawhatchee River

Key species: Spotted bass, largemouth bass, channel catfish, some flathead catfish, bream of various kinds.

Overview: The Choctawhatchee River begins in Alabama and winds its way through southeast Alabama and into the Florida Panhandle before it empties into the Gulf of Mexico by way of beautiful Choctawhatchee Bay just north of Destin, Florida.

Description: After the two main branches of the Choctawhatchee flow together, the river runs for about 170 miles before it reaches the salt water of the Gulf. The Pea River, another good fishing destination, joins the Choctawhatchee and increases its flow considerably. This is not usually a clear and sparkling river. It has a fair silt load at all times along with its tannic stained water from the riverside vegetation, so anglers shouldn't expect much clarity. However, the fishing can be quite good at times, and the wildness of the surrounding area is very attractive. Big trees and lots of wildlife will most likely be seen. Birds in particular like the Choctawhatchee River. Summertime drought conditions can lower the water level to the point that floating is just not possible, so check ahead. Most of the time, though, the water is fine. The state of Alabama maintains launch ramps in Dale and Geneva Counties. Clayhatchee and Newton boat ramps are in Dale County and will work for most small shallow draft boats. Geneva City Park has a good ramp, also.

Even though the Choctawhatchee is a coastal river and flows through primarily flat lands, the river has some quicker than expected runs, so anglers should be aware that a float will not consist of just sitting back and fishing. Some boat handling will be required in places. A number of tributaries feed into the Choctawhatchee; some of them actually have falls and fast flows, and they give much beauty to the river. There are no dams on the river, so anglers should appreciate one of the last free-flowing rivers of any size in the state.

The fishing: Water level and current flow means a lot to anglers on the Choctaw-hatchee River. If the water is too high, as after heavy upstream rains or after a tropical storm, the river is not only unfishable but also very dangerous. Stay off this river in flood conditions; remember, there are no dams to control water run-off. Likewise, in low water conditions, the fishing and floating can be very slow and very tough. There are logjams and obstructions, so low water can become more of a chore than usual. Check with USGS River Gauge online for real-time water conditions: http://waterdate.usgs.gov/al/nwis/uv?2361000.

Bass fishing can be very good. During the spring, both largemouth and spot-ted bass will be found in backwaters where they like to spawn. They can be quite aggressive at this time. When the bass are on the beds, large dark-colored plastic worms fished slowly through downed trees and other structure can be very produc-tive. Also, big spinner baits and buzz baits worked fast and just below the surface can produce big strikes. Try to run these big spinner baits as close to underwater structure as possible. Try to bump the lure into the limbs and banks if you can without getting hung up. Very often bass will hit just as the bait bumps into the branch or comes free from the obstruction; be ready! During the summer and fall, try to plan trips so bass fishing is done early in the day or late; the bite is better than midday. In low-light conditions (during a rain, for example), a fairly large top-water stick bait cast ahead of the boat and worked slowly back can be good for explosive strikes from hunting bass.

Catfishing can be good, especially when there is some current present. Anglers looking for old Mr. Whiskers should use either frozen or fresh shrimp or cut shad fished along deep drop-offs and bluff faces where the current washes food into the wall below the water. A good bet is to catch a hand-size bream and put it on a hook and let it go see what it can find. Some very big catfish are hooked this way; not all of these big ones make it back to the boat, though. There are lots of snags and obstructions in the river.

For the various kinds of bream, it's hard to beat a box of lively crickets. A cane pole works well to precisely drop a cricket with a tiny split-shot sinker into tight and difficult-to-get-to places. A fly rod will work this way, also. If crickets aren't readily at hand, worms will work, too. In the spring and early summer when bream are bed-ding, action can be very fast, and lots of big bream can be collected quickly.

Anglers shouldn't be surprised when other species show up. Freshwater drum are fairly common and are good battlers on light tackle. There are lots of gar in the river, and they can be more than most anglers want to deal with. Also, the Choc-tawhatchee is very important as a spawning and rearing place for Gulf sturgeon, an endangered species. They are almost never hooked, but they sometimes rocket up out of the water, and this can be a real shock when a seventy-five-pound fish takes to the air close to an angler's boat!

Southeast Region

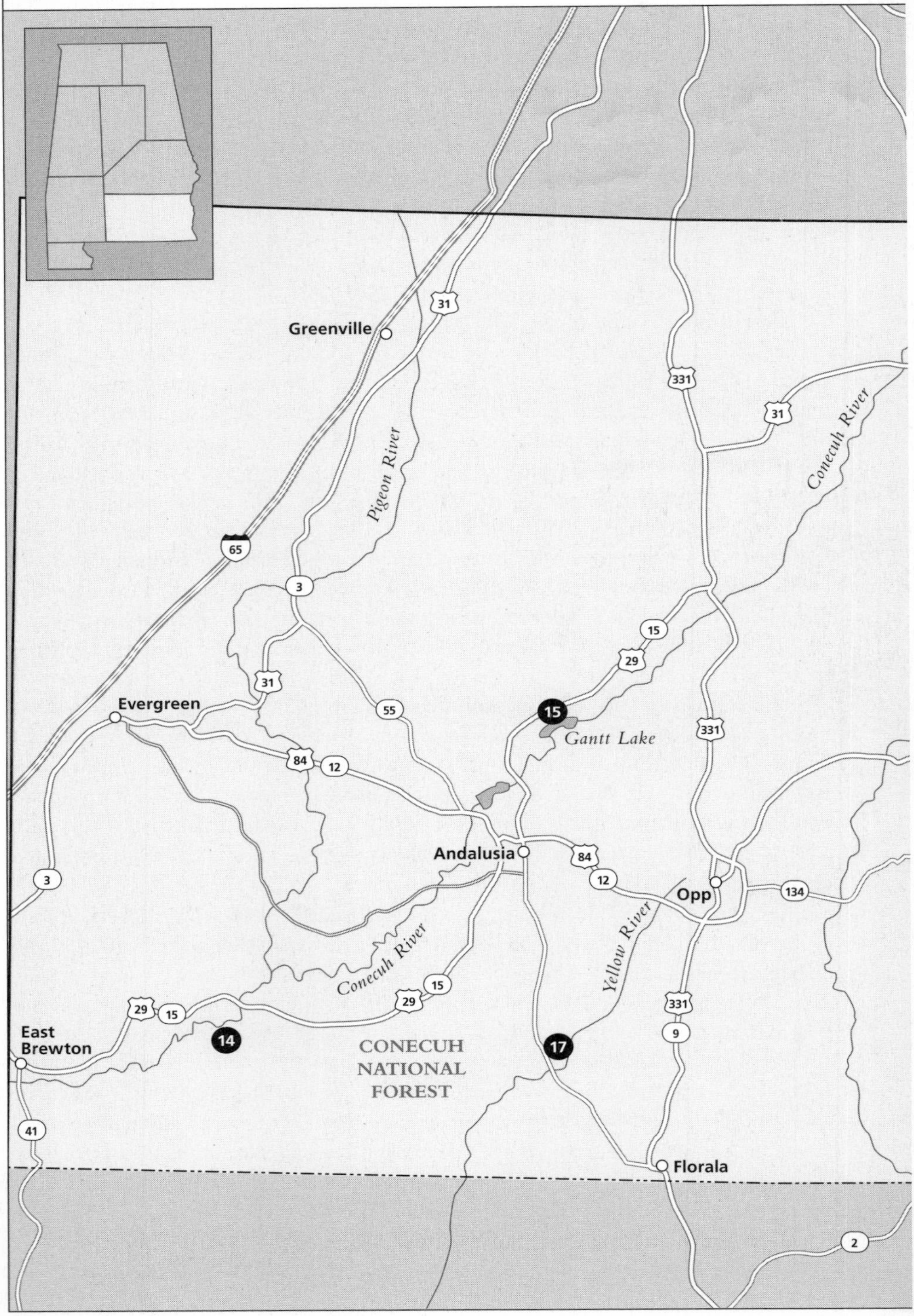

Greenville
Evergreen
Andalusia
Opp
East Brewton
Florala
Gantt Lake
Pigeon River
Conecuh River
Conecuh River
Yellow River
CONECUH NATIONAL FOREST
31
331
31
65
3
15
29
31
55
15
331
84
12
84
12
134
3
29
15
15
29
331
9
14
17
41
2

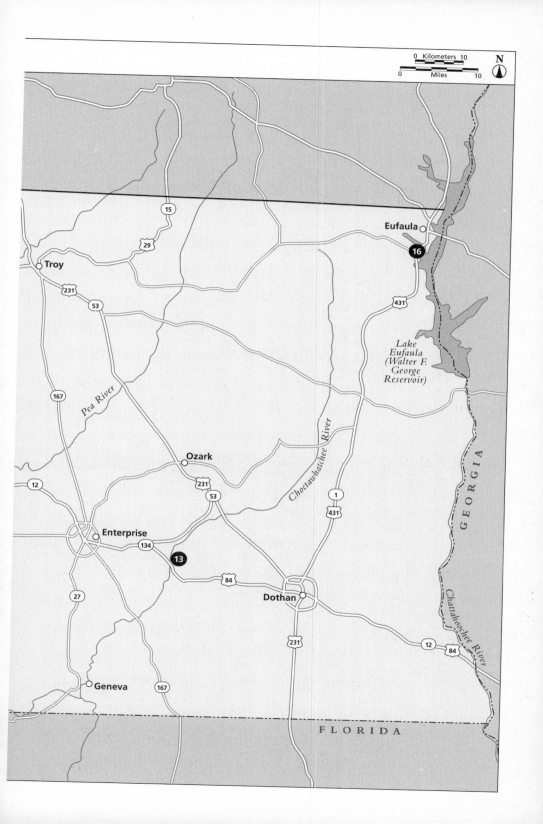

DeLorme: Alabama Atlas & Gazetteer: Page 60 B5, C4, D4.

Camping and lodging: No public camping in the area, but several places to stay can be found in Enterprise, which is close to where most anglers start their floats.

Tips and cautions: For more specific information about overnighting arrangements and water conditions, contact Enterprise Chamber of Commerce, 553 Glover Street, Enterprise 36330; (800) 235-4730.

Directions: From Enterprise, take Highway 134 east about 20 miles to the Newton access point. The highway crosses the river here and gives good access for anglers. For lower regions of the river, take Highway 27 south from Enterprise to Geneva, where the city park offers good access.

For more information: Alabama Wildlife and Freshwater Fisheries Division.

14 Conecuh River

Key species: Big catfish of several species, bass, bream, some seasonal stripers in lower reaches.

Overview: The Conecuh River starts near Union Springs and flows generally southwesterly until it enters Florida, where it becomes the Escambia River and finally empties into Escambia Bay, which is an offshoot of massive Pensacola Bay. Several tributary streams flow into the Conecuh and increase its flow considerably. The river is not fast at any point, but anglers must be aware of underwater obstructions such as downed trees and fallen banks, which can present hazards.

Description: With an overall length of about 230 miles, the Conecuh River drains almost 4,000 square miles in south-central Alabama. The bottom is primarily sandy. There are some very fine high sand banks, which would be great places for floaters to use as swimming holes and overnight camping stops. The source of the river is almost totally groundwater-underground sources. The river is dammed in a couple of places to create lakes, which are good fishing places in their own right. There are some very nice feeder creeks that contribute both water flow and fishing options for anglers. The float down the Conecuh River is not rewarding just for the fishing. Anglers should enjoy seeing wildlife of several kinds; turkey, deer, otter, and alligators are common. The trees and wildflowers can be outstanding during the spring.

The fishing: As in almost every freshwater body in Alabama, largemouth bass are present in the Conecuh River, and sometimes the bass fishing can be very good. Lures that create a lot of noise either on the surface or underwater are good. Topwater prop-type plugs and rattling crankbaits are good. In the spring, buzz baits are good on bass. Anglers have good results with purple plastic worms (about 6 inches in length is good) fished Texas-style with a weedless hook, right at the head of a pool where a run enters the deeper water. Let the worm drift down current from the moving water and then drop off into the hole. Largemouth and spotted bass find this very hard to resist. Bass like to lie up under logs and other cover and then dart out to nab passing meals. Anglers should pay attention to the steep clay bluffs that drop off into deeper water. Work sinking lures along these banks for good bass catches.

A good population of bream of various kinds is in the river, and many anglers work the backwaters and sloughs for bream. Live bait such as crickets and worms always work on the bream. During the spring and early summer, say April through June, if a floater can find a backwater that is about 3 feet deep and off the main channel and its current, it is almost a sure bet that bream will be there in good numbers bedding up. Drop a worm back there and watch the bobber disappear!

However, the real star of the Conecuh River is old Mr. Whiskers. Some very large (thirty- to fifty-pound) flathead catfish are caught every year, and ten- to fifteen-pound catfish are fairly common. The best way to catch the really big cats is to find a good deep hole with some current and anchor up for night fishing. Anglers in Alabama are allowed to use bream as bait if the angler catches the bream on hook and line, and an eating-size bream put on a big hook and sent to the bottom is the best bait for big catfish. This is not the place for light tackle. For the big catfish, eighty-pound line with rods and reels to handle it is in order. An angler may not catch but two or three fish a night this way, but they will be good ones.

Since the Conecuh runs into salt water not too far after it enters Florida, sometimes unusual fish such as sturgeon are seen in the river. There is a good run of striped bass in the lower reaches of the river in the spring.

A very good float of about 4 miles is from County Road 107 to U.S. Highway 84. This should put anglers in contact with just about all of the stars of this fine river.

Big flathead catfish are common in the Conecuh River.

Southeast Region

DeLorme: Alabama Atlas & Gazetteer: Page 57 G9, G10; page 58 F1, F2.

Camping: Camping is possible at Point A Reservoir just 4 miles from Andalusia. A public park there provides boat ramps, camping, and picnic areas.

Tips and cautions: There are several good state-maintained boat ramps on the Conecuh River. Ramps are at River Falls, Brooklyn Road, and Hart's Bridge in Covington County and at Parker Springs and Edward's Bridge Landing in Escambia County.

Directions: To reach the ramps named above, anglers should follow these directions: For River Falls: Take US 84 west of Andalusia about 3 miles. For Brooklyn Road: Take U.S. Highway 29 south from Andalusia; turn right onto County Road 42, and go about 4 miles. For Hart's Bridge: Take US 29 south from Andalusia; turn right onto CR 42, go about 13 miles, and turn left onto Hart's Bridge Road going south. For Edward's Bridge Landing: From Brewton go south on Highway 41. The road crosses the river.

For more information: Alabama Wildlife and Freshwater Fisheries Division; Conecuh National Forest.

15 Gantt Lake

Key species: Largemouth bass, redear sunfish, bluegill, crappie.

Overview: Gantt Lake was built in the 1920s on the Conecuh River to generate electricity. Gantt is normally about 2,700 acres in size with about 21 miles of shoreline.

Description: A public boat ramp is located on U.S. Highway 29 in the Clearview Community. Gantt Lake has been heavily stocked recently with large releases of channel catfish, largemouth bass, and bluegill. White crappie are emerging as a popular target in Gantt, and recently the white crappie population has grown to the point where it is a viable fishery.

The shoreline is now fairly heavily developed, and during the day it sees considerable skiing, swimming, and other boating activities. This high activity may require anglers to work earlier and later and let the skiers have the lake during the midday hours.

The fishing: Structure is the key to success in Gantt. Largemouth bass are taken most often in the grassbeds and sloughs and other backwaters off the main lake body. Cypress trees are a good focal point for bass anglers. Crankbaits are best in the spring when the bass are preparing to spawn. After spring when summer temperatures warm the water, plastic baits worked slowly along the bottom near structure can work well. Some good low-light, top-water fishing for bass can be had by fishing near shoreline structure that is still close to deeper water. Trees and fallen timber are good places to start the bass search. Also, by using weedless worms and plastic frogs, anglers can tempt some of the largest bass to explode from thick cover. Cast these natural-looking offerings into thick cover and work them into open water.

For the various bream species, traditional tackle and bait work well. Worms and crickets will produce good stringers of bream if used on points, over flats, and at the edge of cover. Try to find shallow flats back in creeks during the spring and summer bedding seasons for very fast bream action. Anglers should be able to pick through smaller bream and keep the larger ones for a good old-fashioned fish fry. A fly rod with a fairly large wet fly in dark colors can be loads of fun. Some very large red-eared bream live here, and they respond well to small, dark plastic-tube jigs fished very slowly in about 4 feet of water; they tend to bed a little deeper than bluegills.

To find the crappie, fish deep drop-offs such as old creek channels. Small tube jigs will work, but the most reliable bait for Gantt crappie is live minnows. Fish them deep and slowly. The crappie will be on beds in late February and early March, and they are very easy to catch once an angler has them located. Most beds will be in or near some sort of wooden structure; willow trees and cypress trees are both very good places. For the biggest crappie, try a white rooster tail spinner retrieved as slowly as possible, the spinner blade just barely ticking over, around shallow water wooden structure. You may get hung up from time to time, but sometimes the "hang-up" will head off toward deeper water.

DeLorme: Alabama Atlas & Gazetteer: Page 59 B6.

Gantt bass show good population density.

Camping and lodging: None on-site. Motels are fairly close to the area. Some camping is available at Point A Reservoir.

Tips and cautions: The lake was being drawn down in 2006–07 to expose the bottom for vegetation control and to facilitate some construction projects. Anglers should check current conditions before planning to travel to Gantt.

Directions: From Andalusia, take US 29/Highway 15 north to Gantt Reservoir.

For more information: Alabama Wildlife and Freshwater Fisheries Division.

16 Lake Eufaula (Walter F. George Reservoir)

Key species: Bass, bass, and more bass—largemouth and spotted; crappie, catfish, striped bass, hybrid striped bass.

Overview: Here's a chance for an angler to fish a lake that is a legend. There's probably no bass fishing lake in the world more famous and well-known than Walter F. George/Lake Eufaula. It's known as "the Bass Fishing Capital of the World," and there's reason for that. Largemouth bass grow fast here, and they grow big.

Description: Located on the Chattahoochee River, Lake Eufaula occupies territory in both Alabama and Georgia. Eufaula is large—45,181 acres—and it stretches from Phenix City, Alabama, to Walter F. George Dam at Fort Gaines, Georgia. A nearly 12,000-acre refuge is on the edge of Lake Eufaula, and it helps maintain the quality of the surrounding area.

This is perfect frying-size Eufaula catfish.

When first created, Lake Eufaula had acres and acres of standing dead timber that provided ideal largemouth bass habitat. The cover has gradually deteriorated in the water, but the largemouth are still there, and they have been joined by their cousins, spotted bass, which prefer a more open habitat.

In the past seven years, hydrilla—a fast-growing non-native water weed—has come to dominate parts of the lake. Captain Sam Williams, a quality guide on Eufaula, tells me that the hydrilla has improved fishing. In the summer it shades the water and keeps it cooler. In the winter the hydrilla helps maintain warmth so the bass don't leave the shallower areas of the lake to find comfortable water. There is also a heavy growth of native lily pads and American lotus that offer good cover for the bass.

Anglers will no doubt see alligators when fishing Lake Eufaula. They present no problem. On our last trip there, we had a 4-foot 'gator that followed us around as we fished. No matter where we went in the area, there he was; maybe he was lonely!

Many public access areas such as marinas, parks, and campgrounds have been constructed on or near Lake Eufaula to give residents and visitors easy ways to get on the large lake and partake of its bounty. Many conveniences such as shopping centers, restaurants, and overnight lodgings are close at hand. The town of Eufaula is a good place for non-angling members of the family to explore. The old town is full of Victorian homes in various stages of repair and small shops of many different kinds. There are lots of bait and tackle shops in which anglers can purchase any sort of needed supplies for a visit.

The fishing: Why is the bass fishing so good on Eufaula? There is plenty for the predatory largemouth to eat. Both gizzard shad and threadfin shad populations are very high in Eufaula, and this promotes rapid bass growth. Most anglers who fish Eufaula for largemouth bass use baits that resemble shad. Crankbaits, spinner baits, and silver-colored tube lures take many bass. Bass in Eufaula respond readily to top-water plugs in shad finishes that are "walked" across the water. Captain Sam Williams of Hawks Fishing Guide Service (334-687-6266) says that one of the best baits on Eufaula right now is a plastic frog from Big Bite Baits. The frog should be cast into the lily pads and worked toward open water and pockets in the pads. He says the bass explode on the soft plastic frog.

Since the old wooden structure in Eufaula has gradually rotted away for the most part, the lake's overall habitat has become more to the liking of spotted bass. Spots like a less-cluttered lake, and recent studies have shown the spotted bass population to be really expanding and developing larger individuals. Like the largemouth, which are still here in great numbers, spots love to eat shad, so smart anglers should focus attention on those baits that most resemble silver shad.

In the spring, striped bass and hybrid stripers fill the upper reaches of feeder creeks as they try to spawn. At this time, they are very vulnerable to spoons, jigs, and crankbaits that look like large shad. After the spring spawn, stripers and hybrids can still be readily caught in the main body of the lake as they attack schools of shad on top of the water. Top-water lures in chrome and white finishes can be deadly on schooling stripers.

Although the crappie fishery in Eufaula is not as well-known as the world-famous largemouth fishery, the lake has an excellent population of crappie, and anglers can keep any size crappie. Spring is the classic time to catch big strings of crappie. Fish shoreline structure such as willow and just-emerging lily pads for fast crappie action. Many smart anglers do their crappie fishing at night during the summer. They put out bait-attracting lights and fish minnows fairly deep over submerged structure. This is a great way to wind down from work and get sanity back into your life. Anchor over some good deep structure, put on the lights in the water, drop down a minnow, and perhaps drink a cold iced tea. Now, this is a good ending to any day!

Catfishing can be very good in Eufaula, with both blue and channel catfish common. Catfish in Eufaula respond well to shad on both trot lines and handheld rods. Fishing after dark when most of the noise from skiers and Jet Skis has stopped is a very pleasant way to spend an evening, and it often produces the main ingredient for a Southern fish fry! Another productive method of catfishing in Eufaula is to use jugs to float hooks and baits. It seems that the catfish will rarely allow the angler to finish a set of jugs before having to go and chase down hooked fish!

Bream and other sunfish are present in Eufaula, but they have to compete with the hordes of shad for much of the same food supply, and the shad seem to win most of the time. Sunfish are there, but they tend to run small.

DeLorme: Alabama Atlas & Gazetteer: Page 54 G5, F4, E4, D4, C4.

Camping: Lakepoint Resort State Park is just beside the wildlife refuge, and it's only 7 miles north of the city of Eufaula. Lakepoint has a modern campground, and it also offers twenty-nine cabins and ten lakeside cottages. Excellent ramps are at Lakepoint.

Tips and cautions: Many bass tournaments are held on Lake Eufaula. Unless an angler is taking part in a particular tournament, it might be better or at least easier if he or she went to another part of the lake, rather than the staging area marina or launch ramp for the tournament. A very special bass tournament for anglers is held every year at Lakepoint Marina in June. The Lee King Benefit Tournament raises money to help kids and families with Niemann-Pick Disease, a terminal childhood illness, and offers anglers a chance to help these kids while competing for good cash prizes. Interested anglers should contact Sam Williams at (334) 687-6266 for dates and information. It's a good deal for a good cause!

Directions: From Dothan, take U.S. Highway 431 north. This road will lead directly into Eufala. Traffic can be quite heavy on weekends. Go through the town of Eufala, and direction signs to various parks, marinas, and other facilities will appear. The lake is immediately to the right as you go north and can be seen from the road in many places.

For more information: Alabama Wildlife and Freshwater Fisheries Division.

Good Eats

Captain Sam recommends the Creek Restaurant on U.S. Highway 431 south of Eufaula for its beef tips. He also recommends The Anchor Inn on White Oak Creek for steaks, catfish, and quail. We ate at Phil's Barbeque in Eufaula, and it was very good.

17 Yellow River

Key species: Largemouth bass, bream of various kinds, catfish.

Overview: The Yellow River is typical Gulf Coast blackwater river. The water is usually clear, but it appears dark because of the large amount of tannin in the water from surrounding forested areas. The river can muddy up after a heavy rain, so anglers need to be prepared for changeable water conditions.

Description: There is very little development on the banks of Yellow River. This unusual condition gives anglers a chance to enjoy fishing a river that looks basically the way that all coastal rivers used to look. The river starts near Rose Hill, Alabama, and runs south where it joins Blackwater Bay near Pensacola, Florida. Anglers will very likely see a wide range of wildlife on its banks. Deer, alligators, otters, turkey, and, of course, snakes are common sights along the Yellow River. Spring and fall are particularly nice on the Yellow because of the huge numbers of migrating songbirds that pass through here on their way north and south.

Yellow River bluegills provide great sport on light tackle.

The Yellow River must be floated by a portable boat in many conditions! Log-jams are common and can bring a promising fishing trip to a halt if the boat can't be carried around or pushed over the jam. In dry conditions, the river can be almost unfloatable and unfishable. Also, watch heavy rains. They can bring the water up to dangerous levels quickly. When strong weather is predicted, it might be best to postpone a Yellow River float trip until better conditions prevail.

The fishing: Largemouth bass fishing can be quite good in the Yellow River, but anglers will need to work deeper cover for best results. Weedless rigs are helpful in avoiding constant hang-ups on the brush. Texas-rigged plastic worms are effective on deeper water bass. Try purple and black in fairly large sizes. Soft plastics and spinner baits worked deep and slow can do well. Early and late hours on the river can be very good using top-water baits. Look at sidewaters and sloughs off the main river flow for some good spring bass fishing. Buzz baits and prop baits are all good in low-light conditions.

Bream fishing is good along the Yellow River. Live bait (crickets, worms, and catalpa worms when they can be had) are all good for bluegill, redears, and all other bream species. When bream can be found on beds, the fishing can be excellent. Try drifting an unweighted hook and worm over the shallow water beds to locate the very best parts of the bed for big bream.

Catfishing can be good in deeper holes with some current. Live bream and dead shrimp can be effective catfish bait. Folks who fish the Yellow River a lot use a hand-size bream fished around snags and brush piles to hook up with nice cats. In the lower regions, saltwater species travel up the river, so it is not out of the question for Alabama anglers to encounter the odd redfish or other saltwater species in the Yellow River.

DeLorme: Alabama Atlas & Gazetteer: Page 59 F6, G5.

Camping: Florala State Park (P.O. Box 322, Florala, Alabama 36442; 334-858-6425) offers a campground, swimming, and even some good fishing in the park's Lake Jackson.

Directions: For a good all day float trip, from Florala take Highway 55 north to the Watkins Bridge crossing. Take out about seven to eight hours later at Givens Bridge. The rate of current will determine if the trip takes longer or shorter.

For more information: Alabama Wildlife and Freshwater Fisheries Division; Florala Chamber of Commerce.

East-Central Region

The east-central region of Alabama presents anglers with a wide range of fishing possibilities. Anglers can occupy themselves by chasing big largemouth bass and stripers in big lakes and reservoirs, and they can also fish for spotted bass and float down some mighty pretty streams, too.

Most of the fishing sites in this region are dammed rivers. Even the streams that are fishing destinations here have dams on them, and this means navigating the bodies of water in this part of the state may require a bit more care than usual. Anglers must pay close attention to water levels, and especially when fishing immediately below big dams, they must be aware of water flow conditions. However, when the dams are moving water is when the fish usually bite best.

Another advantage to fishing the east-central region is that a number of large towns are in this area, so supplies and food are never far away.

Finally, some of the most beautiful lakes and streams in the entire state can be found here, and if an angler can't find a place to fish in this region that pleases him or her, then that angler is pretty hard to please!

18 Bartlett's Ferry Reservoir—Lake Harding

Key species: Largemouth bass, spotted bass, hybrid striped bass, striped bass, catfish, crappie.

Overview: Bartlett's Ferry is a nearly 6,000-acre lake on the Alabama-Georgia border. Created when the Chattahoochee River was dammed in 1926, the lake is not as well-known or as heavily fished as its neighboring lakes (Lake Eufaula and West Point Lake).

Description: Although the original wood cover has long since rotted away, Bartlett's Ferry still has plenty of prime fish habitat for anglers to target. Steep bluffs, rocky points, and the original river channel are all good features to work. There is good access to the lake with at least three Alabama-side public ramps at Chattahoochee Valley Recreation Park, Halawakee Creek, and near the dam site. There are several private marinas on the lake to serve angler's needs.

The lake tends to follow the old river channel, and the banks are steep and rocky in many places. The state of Georgia publishes some very good information about Bartlett's Ferry fishing, as it seems to be very popular with Georgia anglers from the Atlanta area.

The fishing: Most anglers at Bartlett's Ferry fish for bass by working boat docks, rocky points, and underwater hills. Spinner baits, crankbaits, and plastics worked along the bottom are good on largemouth bass. Most largemouth caught in Bartlett's Ferry will be three pounds or less, but some larger fish are present. The lake's

East-Central Region

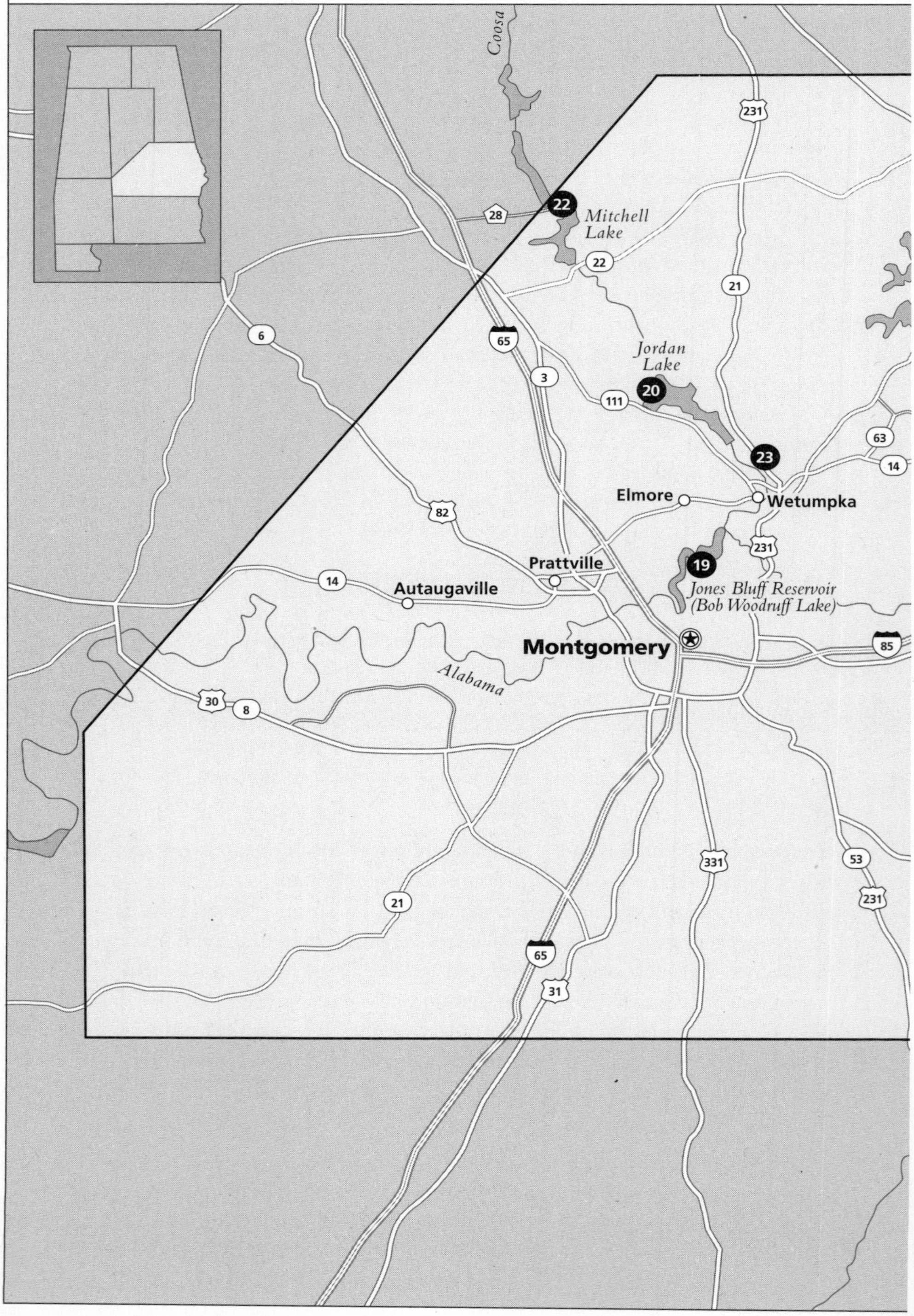

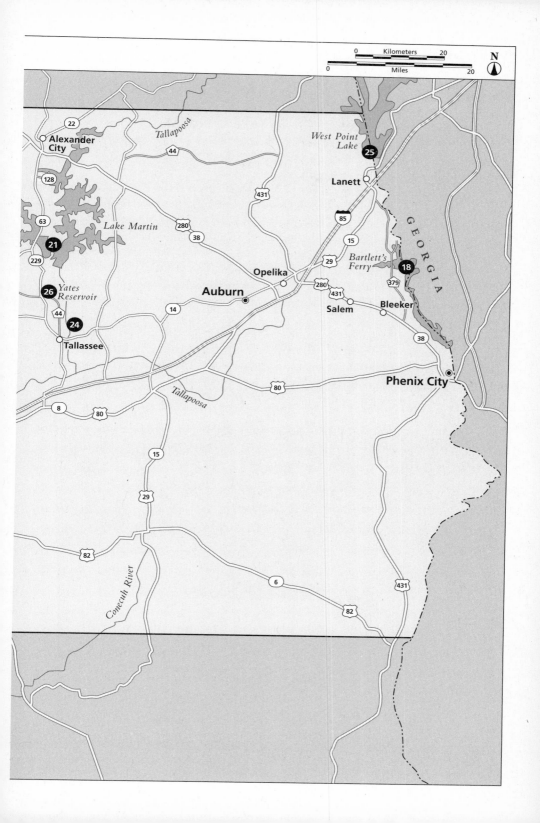

largemouth population seems to be holding fairly steady both in size and numbers, but the same is not true of the lake's spotted bass. The spotted bass population seems to be increasing in Bartlett's Ferry, and these fish tend to be found near rocky areas and old creek and river channels. Spots tend to run small at this time (a foot or less in length), but there are lots of them, and they are great fun to catch. For some fast spotted bass action on Bartlett's Ferry, try a small, dark-colored jig with either a short plastic worm trailer or a small pork rind trailer. Work these baits over humps and drop-offs. The spotted bass love to eat crawfish, and something that closely resembles a craw will surely bring in the spots.

Hybrid bass fishing is good in the lake, and the striper fishery appears to be ready to boom. Gulf-species stripers have been stocked in Bartlett's Ferry, and they seem to be growing very fast and getting very big. Look for these big guys in open water after their spring spawning run. They will be chasing shad in the early morning, and then they will go deeper for afternoon raids on shad that have gone deep out of the sun. Try big silver spoons or deep-running lipped plugs like Red Fins trolled behind sinkers. Fish near the dam and upstream to Riverview Dam during the spring run to find the largest concentration of stripers. Come equipped; they are big.

Crappie are very common, and during their spring spawning season, anglers catch many crappie with small live minnows and small jigs with spinners. A good area to try for crappie is around cypress and gum trees in the lower reaches of the lake. The Georgia Game and Fish folks have put several fish-attracting devices in the lake on the Georgia side, and crappie find these very good places to stay.

A quiet morning on Bartlett's Ferry—for right now.

Finally, catfishing is usually quite good. The common run of channel cats is two to three pounds—just right for filleting. There are bigger cats here, and when going after the big boys, try a large shad for bait and forty-pound test line.

DeLorme: Alabama Atlas & Gazetteer: Page 47 A10.

Camping: It appears that the best camping facilities on the lake are on the Georgia side. Blanton Creek Park is a full-service campground.

Tips and cautions: Anglers fishing Bartlett's Ferry may have either Alabama or Georgia licenses to fish the lake on either side.

Directions: From Opelika take U.S. Highway 280 east. Go through the towns of Salem and Bleeker. Turn north on County Road 379 toward Dupriest Crossroads. Continue north to Mechanicsville. Stay on CR 379 and it will cross the lake.

For more information: Alabama Wildlife and Freshwater Fisheries Division.

19 Jones Bluff Reservoir (Bob Woodruff Lake)

Key species: Largemouth bass, spotted bass, crappie; striped bass and hybrid bass below the dam.

Overview: Jones Bluff is a Corps of Engineer lake that follows the old Alabama River channel. Over 12,500 acres are covered by the lake, which provides navigation and flood control and generates electricity. The lake supports healthy populations of gamefish for anglers and provides good recreation for residents of central Alabama.

Description: This lake demands that anglers work it almost as they would a river. The effects of current are present in the main body. Upstream heavy rains can change the water conditions, such as clarity, temperature, and current, very quickly, so anglers must be flexible. Because the lake is so close to several large population centers such as Montgomery, it gets a lot of pressure during the spring and summer.

The fishing: Jones Bluff has good, reliable largemouth bass fishing in the parts off the main lake body. Creek channels, sloughs, and backwaters are best for largemouths. Spinner and buzz baits are good in the spring; and during summer, plastic baits worked deep and slow near structure pay off. Since there is a good population of small shad in Jones Bluff, silver shad look-alike baits such as spoons, crankbaits, and light-colored jigs work well. Spotted bass seem to prefer the main lake body points and structure where the current is more of an influence. Jones Bluff is one of those lakes that may be better, all things considered, during the winter months. Recreational traffic slows down a whole lot, and the fish still bite well. Bass anglers should continue to use the same types of baits they used during the spring and summer, but just slow down the presentation and work the water just a little bit deeper. Steep bluffs just off the main river channel can be very good in winter. For some big bass, try a dark-colored jig, about one-half ounce, with either bucktail or springy rubber legs and a pork rind trailer. Work this slowly around deep drops and

Jones Bluff largemouths hit hard.

bluffs and along old logs in deep water and see what happens. Some very nice bass are caught this way every year.

The crappie fishery is quite good in Jones Bluff, and anglers who drop small, light-colored jigs and live minnows into deeper structure (10 to 15 feet) can gather heavy stringers of tasty crappie. Of course, in spring the speckled slabs seek shallow water to spawn, and anglers must follow their movement. Look up feeder creeks for shallow flats to find springtime crappie.

Below Henry Lock and Dam, anglers who chase hybrids and stripers do quite well in the spring when the fish gather in the tailrace of the dam. White jigs and heavy spoons that can be worked deep in the fast currents are good for spring stripers. Anglers from boat and bank do very well when the hybrids and stripers gang up at the tailrace waters.

Catfish anglers can catch some very big fish by drifting live shad downstream toward logjams and other permanent structure. The biggest cats will usually be found in places where there is some current, and they like to have deep water and some sort of bottom structure close at hand. For the smaller channel catfish "fiddlers," try prepared catfish baits and live minnows fished in more open areas.

DeLorme: Alabama Atlas & Gazetteer: Page 44 D3.

Camping: In Prattville, Cooter's Pond has about forty trailer spots and a boat launch.

South of the lake, Gunter Hill has nearly 150 campsites, and Prairie Creek Campground has almost 70 campsites, fish cleaning stations, and boat launch facilities.

Tips and cautions: Since Jones Bluff has an almost constant current flow, it does not temperature stratify nearly as much as most lakes in summer. This can make patterning fish more difficult as they tend to be more scattered than usual in lakes.

Directions: From Interstate 65 north of Montgomery, take Highway 14 west through Prattville. Go through Autaugaville on Highway 14. Turn south on County Road 8 before reaching Mulberry. At Peace, take County Road 9 to the lake.

For more information: Alabama Wildlife and Freshwater Fisheries Division.

20 Jordan Lake

Key species: Spotted bass, largemouth bass, hybrid striped bass, bream, crappie, catfish.

Overview: Jordan Lake was impounded in 1928 for electricity generation, but it has created a popular recreational site for many central Alabama residents and visitors.

Description: Twenty-five miles north of Alabama's capital city, Jordan Lake is a nearly 7,000-acre lake created by the impoundment of the Coosa River. The original dam was finished in 1928, but the connecting Bouldin Dam was brought online in

Lake Jordan's shoreline has light residential development.

1967. Bonner's Point and Rotary Landing are on opposite sides of the lake and offer good access to anglers coming from either north or south. By the way, the name of the lake is pronounced "Jer-dan."

The lower parts of the lake near the dam are deep, and there are few shallow flats in this region. Toward the upper areas of the lake, the water is shallower and several feeder creeks and streams broaden the habitat possibilities for gamefish. Private marinas and several public boat ramps and launch areas give good access to Jordan Lake. The Bouldin Canal, which connects to Jordan Lake, leads to Bouldin Dam, which generates electricity, and when the dam is pumping and current flows through the canal, it can trigger feeding by gamefish in the immediate area.

The fishing: For spotted bass, Jordan may be the best lake in the state. The deeper rock structured bottom of Jordan toward the dam creates the perfect spotted bass habitat. Spotted bass respond well to shad imitation lures, spinner baits, and plastic baits, but the best results on spotted bass come from crawfish imitations. Crank-baits are very effective when used around rock and boulder structure. Points running out into the main lake body are particularly good spots to look for spotted bass in Jordan. Largemouth are present, but they tend to locate themselves farther uplake toward the tributary streams, where more shallow areas with plenty of wood, downed trees, and flood debris create places more suitable for bigmouths. After spring spawning is completed, Jordan bass, especially largemouth, orient themselves to grass beds where they find shade, cooler water, and concealment. These areas are good summer and fall areas to explore.

Good populations of shad provide forage for stripers and hybrids in the open waters. To target Jordan stripers, hybrids, and whites, try light-colored crankbaits; just vary the sizes for the specific species. Bigger baits should be used for the stripers, middle-size for the hybrids, and smaller (one-quarter to one-half ounce) for the whites. However, don't be surprised when the biggest striper hits the smallest bait. These rapid movers are hard to pattern, and they don't always follow an angler's plan. During the summer, try dropping live shad down to deep concentrations of stripers, which show up well on fish-finder screens. Also, below the dam in the spring, good runs of stripers and hybrids congregate in the pools below the dam. Striper and hybrids show up in the tailrace waters year-round.

Look for crappie around deep water in the summer. Try small jigs worked vertically through the depths in standing timber areas. It may take awhile to locate the crappie and their preferred depth, but once found, they usually stay put. Live minnows fished on a small, one-sixteenth-ounce jig head are good to find the crappie. Of course, during the spring run, crappie will be up in creek channels looking for shallow water to spawn in.

DeLorme: Alabama Atlas & Gazetteer: Page 45 A8.

Camping: Lake Jordan Marina has a few campsites. Shoal Creek Bridge (334-391-4778) also has campsites.

Tips and cautions: Alabama Power Company provides more information about fish habitat enhancement coordinates at www.southernco.com/hydro/home.asp.

Directions: From Montgomery take Interstate 65 north. Take exit 181 east onto Highway 14. Continue on Highway 14 through Elmore into Wetumpka. From Wetumpka take Highway 111 north. Signs to the dam site and other access points will be on the right side of the road.

For more information: Alabama Wildlife and Freshwater Fisheries Division.

21 Lake Martin

Key species: Largemouth bass, spotted bass, striped and hybrid striped bass, several species of catfish.

Overview: Lake Martin was constructed in 1926 when the Alabama Power Company dammed the Tallapoosa River near the Elmore/Tallapoosa County line. At the time, the lake was built to control floods and to generate electrical power, but it has become one of Alabama's premier recreational lakes.

Description: Covering nearly 40,000 acres with over 700 miles of shoreline, Lake Martin has many access facilities, which give anglers a wide range of choices to use. The lake is well-mapped, and these topo maps can make the job of locating fish structure much easier. There are a number of very attractive feeder streams that present many additional angling opportunities at Lake Martin.

This is great bait to use on Lake Martin spotted bass.

This is truly one of the most attractive lakes in Alabama, or anywhere else, for that matter. In fact, much of the time when we read or hear about Lake Martin, the word "beautiful" is used before the name so often, it almost seems to be part of the name. This really is a great place to visit.

Lake Martin has clear water and rocky, steep banks. Much of the bottom is small rock and gravel. This makes for a very good spotted bass fishery, but it also makes the lake harder than most lakes in Alabama to fish. Compared to Guntersville, Weiss, and Eufaula, Lake Martin is infertile, but this does not mean that there are no fish. There are plenty of fish here, and some very good ones. However, the equipment and techniques used at some of the other lakes will need to be modified for best results at Lake Martin. The lake's waters are not as colored as the other major lakes, and this requires anglers to scale down in tackle; light spinning gear is best. The fish in Lake Martin tend to run somewhat smaller in size when compared to other Alabama lakes. However, the sheer beauty of this hill country lake and its shoreline and clear water make the difference acceptable to most anglers. Lake Martin is a very popular recreational destination, and lots of folks visit it during the season.

The fishing: When fishing for bass in Lake Martin, think light tackle. Ten-pound test line should be adequate for most bass fishing situations. The bass population here is heavily tipped in favor of spotted bass over their largemouth cousins. The

Fine ramps and facilities are found at Wind Creek.

whole environment of the lake just seems to favor spots. There are bigmouths, of course, but the spots just seem to beat them to anglers' baits most of the time. Compared to most other Alabama lakes, Lake Martin is a good year-round fishing destination. In fact, winter may be better than the middle of summer for fishing. Spotted bass in particular tend to school up and chase shad during winter months, and this can be a very exciting time to fish. During the summer, Lake Martin gets a great deal of Jet Ski, ski boat, and other noisy boat traffic, which disrupts the fishing. The best time to fish Lake Martin during the summer is at night when everything calms and quiets down.

Spotted bass orient to the steep bluffs of the main lake while largemouth bass tend to stay in the shallower creek channels and other backwaters off the main body. This is a very good lake for "finesse" fishing. Anglers serious about catching a good mess of bass should think of small slider-type plastic worms with one quarter ounce or so jig heads fished very slowly around steep bluffs and gravel bottom. Some of the newer "scented" plastic worms are very good for this technique. Lake Martin is not the place for big and noisy lures, most of the time. Of course, when the bass are actively chasing shad in open water, all bets are off. At this time, anglers should use something that is heavy enough to be thrown a long way, and shiny enough to match the shad and catch a hungry bass's attention. Since there is a good shad population in the lake, shad imitations in chrome, white, and chartreuse are good for both spotted and largemouth bass. During the cold months, look for spotted bass to school in large groups as they chase shad in the main lake body.

Crappie are very good in Lake Martin, and they can be caught around stumps and downed tree limbs along the shoreline. Small, dark-colored jigs, spinners, and live minnows gather up the crappie. Look for crappie up major feeder creeks near fallen timber in the water. Try small, light-colored jigs tipped with a small minnow around brush piles. You may hang up some and lose some jigs, but you will also catch some of the biggest crappie around this way. Scientific surveys done on the crappie here indicate that the lake is pretty much full of black crappie, and that the crappie fishery should be very strong for years to come.

Striped bass are best located in deep water by using fish finders, or by watching for them as they chase shad on top in the open waters of the lake. They do like shiny top-water baits when they chase shad in open water. When fishing for the stripers that are fairly common here, line weight and equipment should be stepped up accordingly. There are plenty of stripers in Lake Martin that will not be stopped by ten-pound line. A good level-wind casting reel on a 6-foot medium-heavy rod with fifteen- to twenty-pound test line is about right. There are some gorgeous feeder creeks that run into Lake Martin, and during the spring, they can be super-hot for spawning white bass, hybrids, and even a few stripers.

DeLorme: Alabama Atlas & Gazetteer: Page 39 E7, F7,G7, H7.

Camping: This is a very strong point of Lake Martin. Some of the best campgrounds this writer has ever seen are to be found here. In particular, Wind Creek State Park is fantastic. It is the largest state-owned campground in the United States: 626 separate campsites. Great camping spots near the lake, a very good launch area, and a full-range camp store with laundry facilities make Wind Creek a fine place to spend a few days. Many bass tournaments are held with Wind Creek as the starting and check-in point. There are also facilities at Sandy Creek, Madwind Creek, Kowaliga Creek, and Pace's Point close to Camp Alamisco.

Directions: From Alexander City, take Highway 63 south about 7 miles. Turn left onto Highway 128.

For more information: Alabama Wildlife and Freshwater Fisheries Division.

22 Mitchell Lake

Key species: Largemouth bass, spotted bass, bream of several kinds, crappie.

Overview: Created in 1922 with the damming of the Coosa River, Mitchell Lake is nearly 6,000 acres in coverage and nearly 150 miles of shoreline. At the upper end of the lake, the Lay Lake tailrace waters are quite popular, especially with shore anglers. Mitchell Lake is a relatively fertile body of water, and its gamefish show good growth and size when compared to other Alabama lakes.

Description: Ten miles east of the central Alabama town of Clanton, Mitchell Lake has public and private boat ramps and marinas for anglers to gain access to the

Crappie this size are perfect for filleting and frying up right!

water. Mitchell does show some periodic rise and fall in size and number of fish populations, but it never seems to fall drastically to unacceptable angling levels. The Alabama Wildlife and Freshwater Fisheries have stocked Mitchell Lake fairly heavily since the 1980s. Stocked species include walleye, striped bass, and hybrid striped bass. The success of these stocked species remains to be seen, but they are in the lake.

The fishing: Mitchell Lake appears to be a spring- and fall-oriented lake. Although anglers do well in all seasons, the spring and fall tend to produce more and better fish. During the spring, crappie anglers do very well when the big slabs move into shallow water around shoreline trees and brush to spawn. Small jigs, beetle-spins, and, of course, live minnows produce many heavy strings of crappie.

Bream are best sought near shallow water sloughs and weedy backwaters. Worms, crickets, and popping bugs on fly rods are good ways to collect some tasty sunfish. There are good catfish populations in Mitchell Lake, so don't be surprised if something big and whiskery tries to take off with your bream rig.

Largemouth bass tend to congregate around the stretches of willow-covered shoreline. Big spinner baits tossed around the heavy fallen limb cover under the willows are good baits in the springtime. Later, fish the backwaters and sloughs with soft plastics worked slowly on the bottom.

Striped bass tend to be found in humps and points in the main lake body. Try shad imitations for the spotted bass.

DeLorme: Alabama Atlas & Gazetteer: Page 37 F10.

Camping: Free boat launch, campsites, RV sites, and other facilities are available at Higgens Ferry Park, (205) 755-5952.

Directions: From Clanton, take Interstate 65 south to U.S. Highway 31/Highway 3/Highway 22. Follow US 31/Highway 3/Highway 22. Turn left onto Highway 22, which will lead to the lower lake area.

For more information: Alabama Wildlife and Freshwater Fisheries Division; Alabama Power Company.

23 Lower Coosa River

Key species: Spotted bass, largemouth bass, various bream, striped bass.

Overview: The Coosa River runs from Georgia to nearly Montgomery, Alabama. It is dammed at various locations on its route. The section between the tailrace of Jordan Dam and the town of Wetumpka downstream, about 10 miles by stream, offers anglers some excellent fishing opportunities.

Description: Generally clear and featuring good current, the Lower Coosa is an excellent float stream for both johnboats and canoes and kayaks. Anglers do need to exercise caution because there are numerous shoals and some rapids that demand respect. There are some Class III rapids, which can be a problem in some condi-

Jordan Dam is the start of the Lower Coosa.

tions. This is one body of water for which an angler needs to use a guide for the first trip or two to become familiar with the river.

When power is being generated at Jordan Dam, anglers should be particularly careful of rapid water and strong currents. The Coosa can be dangerous in high-water conditions. Small craft can be carried very carefully from the Jordan Dam site to the river for floating, but the trail to the river from the overlook park is steep and long. Most anglers will launch downstream and motor or paddle up. Certain weekends have very popular festivals on the river, and anglers would do best to avoid fishing the Coosa on these weekends. The most commonly fished stretch of the river from Jordan Dam to Wetumpka is about 7.5 miles.

The fishing: All of the lakes in the Coosa chain of dammed lakes have good spotted bass fisheries. Those spotted bass had to come from somewhere, and that somewhere is the natural Coosa River. Population studies conducted by the state show that spotted bass are thick in the Lower Coosa, and they are bigger than the usual Alabama spotted bass. Scientists account for this because the Lower Coosa is not as heavily fished as most bodies of water in the state, and because many anglers who do fish the stream don't keep their spotted bass catch. Soft plastics that resemble crawfish are good for spotted bass, as are shad imitations. Spotted bass like to orient themselves to large boulders and other current breaks. Largemouth bass are present in the Coosa, and they tend to be found off the main current areas in sloughs and slower current areas. These largemouth bass are often caught on spinner baits worked near structure. Anglers generally have their best catches in the deeper areas of the river between shoals, rapids, and runs.

There is a very good striped bass fishery in the Lower Coosa, especially in the early spring when the big stripers run upstream toward the Jordan Dam tailwaters where the dam stops their travels. Large silver spoons and light-colored soft jigs are good on the spring stripers. Stripers are caught in the deeper pools below shoals and runs year-round, and they can put a severe strain on equipment and anglers.

DeLorme: Alabama Atlas & Gazetteer: Page 45 B8.

Camping: Fort Toulouse-Jackson Park (334-567-3002) offers camping in a nice secluded setting overlooking the river. In Wetumpka itself, Coosa River Adventures (415 Company Street; 334-514-0279) offers primitive camping for anglers who use the company's services.

Tips and cautions: The city of Wetumpka and the state provide a good ramp and launch area at Crommelin's Landing, which is also known as Golden Park. Anglers with outboard powered boats could motor from this ramp upstream and then float back down to the ramps. Further information can be obtained from Wetumpka Chamber of Commerce.

Directions: From Montgomery, take Interstate 65 north. Turn right onto Highway 14. Go east to the city of Wetumpka. Take Highway 14 Bypass to Highway 231.

Stream bass pull hard. In-line spinners attract them.

Turn right on Highway 231 South, then turn right on Company Street. The access is less than a mile.

For more information: Alabama Wildlife and Freshwater Fisheries Division; Alabama Power Company; Wetumpka Chamber of Commerce.

24 Thurlow Reservoir

Key species: Largemouth bass, spotted bass, striped bass, crappie, large bream.

Overview: Thurlow is not a big lake—only 585 acres coverage—but it offers anglers a chance to get away from crowds of people and still have a good probability of catching some good fish. Located near Tallassee, Thurlow Reservoir is the smallest of the Alabama Power Company's impoundments.

Description: Because of the cooler water discharged from upstream Martin Dam, the water flowing into Thurlow is somewhat infertile when compared to other Alabama lakes, and this affects the growth and numbers of forage fish such as shad. Although this somewhat reduces the amount of food fish for bass and stripers, fishing in Thurlow is usually quite good, probably because the lake does not get heavy fishing pressure. Thurlow is a good place to go to find some good fish without a lot of company.

The fishing: Fishing for largemouth and spotted bass is good. Largemouth seem to be found in shallower water near structure. Sloughs, feeder creek channels, and shorelines with cover such as fallen trees, limbs, and docks are good bets for largemouth. They respond well to standard crankbaits and lipless crankbaits such as Hot Spots and other baits that have a tight, rapid wiggle when retrieved quickly. Shad colors are good. Spotted bass will be found on deeper structure in the main lake body, but they sometimes show up in creek channels and in open water where they chase shad. Watch for schooling bass in open water in late summer and early fall as these fish, which are fattening up for winter, chase shad with abandon.

Stripers and white bass stay in the cooler waters of the main lake body until spring, when they run upstream to spawn. Anglers make some outstanding white bass/hybrid striper catches in the far upstream reaches of the lake near Martin Dam. When the dam is pumping water, the fish congregate in areas of less current (behind rocks and in deeper pockets) where they pick off shad and other bait being swept downstream. Casting a white or chartreuse soft body jig into these slack current areas is very good.

Thurlow is a very good panfish lake. Anglers who fish live bait such as worms and crickets catch some very large bluegill and redear bream. Look for backcreek areas with shallow flats in the spring and summer. The fat bream will be on the flats bedding, and they respond well to tiny jigs and spinners moved slowly through the bedding area.

DeLorme: Alabama Atlas & Gazetteer: Page 46 B2.

Streams that flow into major lakes are always worth some attention.

Camping: The city of Tallassee operates a park that has a boat ramp, restrooms, picnic area, and a boardwalk, which is wheelchair accessible.

Tips and cautions: Not many bass tournaments are held on Thurlow, so fishing pressure is relatively light.

Directions: From Montgomery, take Interstate 85 to the Highway 229 exit. Go north on Highway 229 to Tallassee. Access to Thurlow is at a city-maintained park just off Gilmer Avenue.

For more information: Alabama Wildlife and Freshwater Fisheries Division.

25 West Point Lake

Key species: Spotted bass, largemouth bass, hybrid stripers, white bass, crappie.

Overview: Covering about 25,000 acres, West Point is a large lake located on the Alabama-Georgia border, with most of the lake in Georgia.

Description: Being so close to metropolitan Atlanta, West Point has suffered through the years from water pollution, but Atlanta has been doing a better job lately of sewage treatment, so the fertility problems have been improved. This both improves water clarity and condition, and the amount and condition of gamefish

Working a shoreline for bass is a good technique.

forage such as shad. West Point Lake is influenced by power generation. When water is released from the dam, fishing gets better because of the current created in the lake.

Alabama fishing licenses are valid in all of the lake except the area north of Georgia Highway 109 Bridge. Most of the lake's access points are located in Georgia. The Corps of Engineers has more than thirty access points to West Point Lake.

The fishing: Spotted bass fishing has become very good recently with the improved water quality. There is a 14-inch minimum length for largemouth, but there is no length limit for spotted bass, and anglers are encouraged to catch and keep smaller spotted bass. Largemouth like to lie in shallower waters such as backwater sloughs and swamps, and they tend to orient around docks, fallen timbers, and other shallower water structure. Soft plastics and early and late top-water baits can be very good. Spotted bass are found just about everywhere, but the bigger fish tend to be deeper around main lake points and underwater hills. Crankbaits and spinner baits work well on spotted bass.

Crappie can be very good in the spring when the fish go shallow and up creeks to spawn.

White bass and stripers in West Point follow the typical pattern for the species. Find them in deeper main lake areas, where they chase shad during most of the year, and up feeder streams during the spring where they go to spawn.

DeLorme: Alabama Atlas & Gazetteer: Page 40 D3.

Camping: Many camping areas can be found around West Point, but most are in Georgia.

Tips and cautions: Interested anglers can find interactive maps of West Point Lake at http://westpt.sam.usace.army.mil/.

Directions: From Montgomery, take Interstate 85 toward Atlanta. Turn north on Highway 15 at Lanett. West Point Lake is literally on the state line.

For more information: Alabama Wildlife and Freshwater Fisheries Division; U.S. Army Corps of Engineers.

26 Yates Reservoir

Key species: Largemouth bass, spotted bass, crappie, striped bass, catfish, yellow perch.

Laurie has a fine bull blue gill taken on a small artificial lure.

Overview: Built in 1928 to provide navigation and electric generation, Yates Reservoir has developed into a reliable fishing destination. It's not a huge lake (1,980 acres in coverage), but many anglers fish Yates with good results.

Description: Yates is another of the fine fishing lakes on the dammed Tallapoosa River. Many locals call Yates "Middle Pond" since it's located between Lake Martin and Lake Thurlow. Both upstream and downstream power generation can influence what happens in Yates Reservoir, so anglers must be aware of what the generation status is. In general, fish bite better when the water is moving through the lake.

The fishing: Forage fish such as shad are not as populous as in some of the other Alabama lakes since the cool water discharged from Martin Lake Dam suppresses shad growth. However, the bass survival in Yates is good, and the bass seem to be very healthy. Some very respectable bass come from Yates Lake every year. Largemouth seem to strongly orient toward backwaters and shallower structure. Soft plastics fished deep work well. Don't be surprised if spotted bass and largemouth come to hand from the same area. Both species in Yates like to hang around deeper creek channels.

Crappie fishing is very good during the spring. Fish shallow willow trees and other fallen cover with live minnow and tiny beetle-spins to collect big slab crappie.

A somewhat unusual fishery is developing in Yates Reservoir with the yellow perch. These smaller panfish are very good eating, and they respond well to small live bait such as worms and sometimes crickets.

Yates has a good population of big stripers. Anglers have a good chance of hooking twenty-pound or larger stripers. Anglers need to exercise caution when fishing the upper reaches of Yates Reservoir because it is very rocky, and currents can be strong when Martin Dam is pumping water.

DeLorme: Alabama Atlas & Gazetteer: Page 46 B2.

Camping and lodging: None in the immediate area. The best bet for overnighting is either to stay in a motel in Tallassee or try campgrounds at some of the nearer lakes.

Tips and cautions: Alabama Power Company maintains two launch ramps on Yates Lake. The Damsite Park has a good ramp, parking, and picnic area. A small ramp is maintained on the Coon Creek Tract by the state of Alabama.

Directions: From Tallassee, take County Road 44 north about 3 miles to the Yates Dam entrance road.

For more information: Alabama Wildlife and Freshwater Fisheries Division; Alabama Power Company.

West-Central Region

The west-central region of Alabama is a land of big rivers, big lakes, and good fishing. Anglers who fish this area generally look for largemouth bass and panfish. However, the catfishing can't be overlooked in west-central Alabama. Anglers going after the big river cats should be sure to come equipped for strong fish that live in obstruction-filled water. Learning the big river–based lakes can take some time and experiences, but most anglers who fish here come to appreciate the hot fishing that often occurs.

Most of the lakes in this region are conveniently located near towns, so obtaining replacement equipment, fuel, and other supplies is never much of a chore. Good access to the fishing lakes is present on all of the covered locations.

Finally, in the fall of the year, anglers in the west-central region could go fishing in the morning and then go to a football game in Tuscaloosa in the afternoon or evening. Now that would be living just about the best possible life in Alabama!

Let's look at the fishing locations in west-central Alabama.

27 Bankhead Reservoir

Key species: Largemouth bass, spotted bass, hybrid striped bass, crappie.

Overview: Originally impounded in 1916, Bankhead has not outlived its productivity. Even though pollution from industrial and municipal sources have in the past diminished Bankhead's quality, the water quality and surroundings have lately been improving, and fishing has not seemed to suffer at all.

Description: Bankhead is the second largest lake on the Warrior River. It is located 15 miles west of Birmingham and about 30 miles northeast of Tuscaloosa. A typical river-system lake, Bankhead has commercial barge traffic that must be monitored by anglers. A major tributary, Valley Creek, is a good fishing destination in itself, and it warrants fishing time. A considerable amount of wood structure (stumps, blown-down trees, and flood debris) makes plenty of fishable cover for anglers to work.

A bit over 9,000 acres in size, the lake is usable for more than 10 miles. Bankhead is kept at near normal pool levels year-round, but during spring the water level can fluctuate somewhat in response to rainfall. Heavy rains can cause the lake to leave its normal boundaries, which tends to scatter gamefish and make them somewhat more difficult to locate.

The fishing: Bankhead has some big bass. Anglers should work visible structure with fairly heavy tackle; twenty-pound line is not too much. A variety of soft plastics such as worms, lizards, and tube will attract big bass. Buzz baits worked around grass beds, lily pads, and other structure can be quite effective on largemouths.

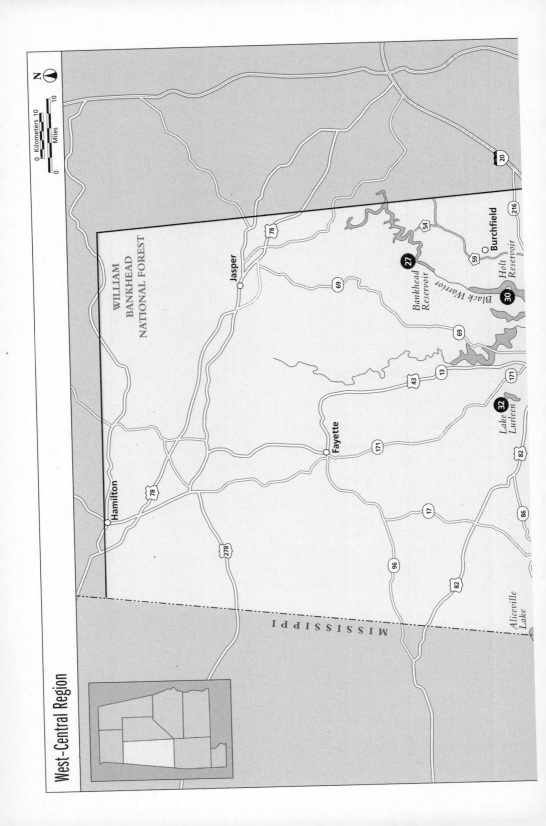

West-Central Region

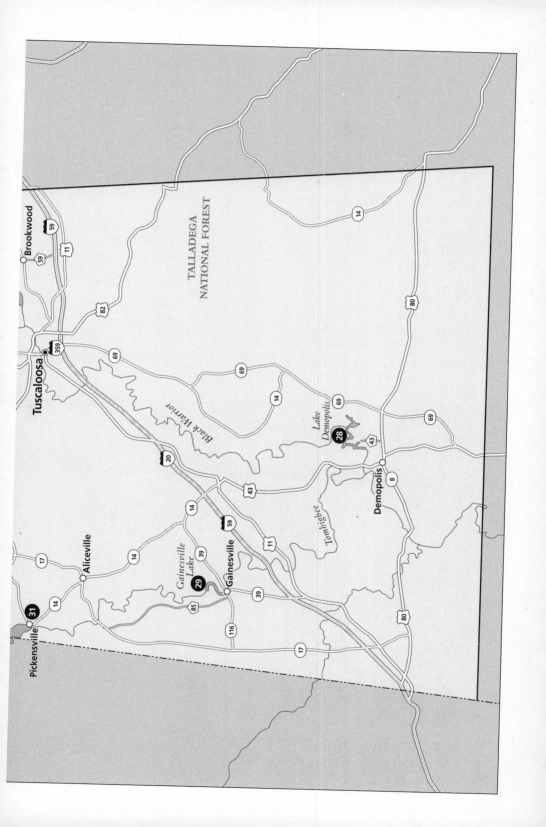

Don't be too eager to move from promising territory. Lots of folks fish Bankhead, so the bass see lots of baits. It may take more than one presentation to tempt the better bass to bite. When rocky structure and steep bluffs are found, spotted bass should be near. Work jigs and crankbaits in crawfish patterns around this hard structure, and spotted bass should result. Don't neglect the flats in the main lake itself. Very often, shad in huge schools will gather on the flats, and the bass will follow them. When bass are chasing shad, top-water baits such as Devil's Horse, Red Fins, and Super Spooks can provide some very exciting strikes.

Crappie grow big in Bankhead, and they tend to relate to structure such as sunken trees and deeper cliffs and bluffs. Small minnow and one-quarter- to one-sixteenth-ounce tube jigs in light colors can be very effective. When spring fishing crappie, try to find a deeper creek off the main lake body that has some fairly shallow water—about 5 feet is good—and cast minnows under small bobbers near structure. The bobber will help keep the minnow out of the brush so the crappie can find it. Once the crappie are located, usually anglers can fish in their preferred manner, and the crappie will start rolling in.

Finally, don't forget the stripers, especially in spring when they run up Smith River to spawn. Some 25-plus-pound stripers have come out of Bankhead. Anglers who go specifically after Bankhead stripers should have a good level-wind reel with a strong and smooth drag system spooled up with twenty-five- to thirty-five-pound

Here's what we're after! Top-water bass!

line. There can be a number of boats fishing a relatively small area, so patience and good manners are important. These spring-run stripers love to eat shad and shad look-alikes. Good results occur when anglers are able to cast live shad hooked through the lips behind the boat and drift down current trailing the bait behind. Use just enough weight to sink the shad near the bottom.

DeLorme: Alabama Atlas & Gazetteer: Page 29 E10, F10.

Camping: A picnic/day-use facility is at the dam site. All other facilities are privately owned.

Tips and cautions: Bankhead gets fairly heavy use during weekends, so if you can schedule fishing trips during the week, you'll find the competition is much less. Summer recreational traffic can be very high since the lake is so close to major cities.

Directions: From Tuscaloosa go east on Interstate 59. Take exit 86 to Brookwood, and from there take County Road 59. Signs to Burchfield Park will lead you to County Road 54 and the lake access.

For more information: Alabama Wildlife and Freshwater Fisheries Division; U.S. Army Corps of Engineers.

28 Lake Demopolis

Key species: Largemouth bass, crappie, hybrid striped bass, bream.

Overview: Stretching for 48 miles up the Black Warrior River and more than 50 miles up the Tombigbee from the dam near the town of Demopolis, Lake Demopolis covers more than 10,000 acres. This is a very popular body of water for both boat anglers and shore anglers. Several access points are provided on both shores of the lake.

tion: Largemouth bass fishing is the premier attraction of Lake Demopolis. In to the good fishing in the lake itself, the tailwaters below Warrior Dam, an up branch of Lake Demopolis, is very popular with local anglers during the spring runs. The tailwater area below Gainesville Dam is a hot spot for catfish anglers. Good shore access is provided at this spot.

The fishing: For bass, the standard reliable plastic baits such as worms, grubs, and large tube jigs are effective. In the spring, fishing large crankbaits and large spinner baits near cover such as downed trees and floating logs can be very good. A 14-inch minimum length requirement for bass should help increase the number of larger bass taken. Night fishing on Demopolis can be very good in hot weather months. Anglers should work shallow points that project into the main lake body by casting large, dark (black is best) top-water lures. Lures that make a bit of noise are good, but don't get carried away with the commotion. Let the top-water lure sit silently after some movement. That quiet pause is often when the bass hit.

Big bull bluegill will take small crankbaits readily.

To catch the largest number and largest size of bream, anglers should work small waters—creeks, streams, backwaters—off the main lake body. Look for areas with good overhanging trees and bushes to help concentrate bream. In the spring when the big bull bream are bedding, anglers should look for shallow (3 feet deep is good) flats where the bream can occupy spawning beds. It may take a little work and looking to find the bream, but once located, the bite will come fast and furious. Tiny jigs can work well for bream, but most anglers rely on worms and crickets. Don't be at all surprised if something grabs your light bream rig and tries to take it from you. There are some large catfish in Lake Demopolis, and they eat the same things that bream do.

During the spring, if the river is not running too high, the upstream waters below the dam at Warrior can produce some outstanding striper and hybrid fishing. Anglers need to exercise care in all tailrace situations; the water level can change very quickly. These big stripers are looking for big shad, and if live shad can be netted, they are the best bait. Anglers should be prepared to lose some tackle on the bottom rocks and other structure, but it should be worthwhile when one of the big striped fish grabs the shad and goes the other way!

DeLorme: Alabama Atlas & Gazetteer: Page 42 B3.

Camping: Forkland Parking Camping Area has forty-two sites with electrical and water hookups. A laundry is on-site.

Tips and cautions: Call (334) 289-5535 to speak with reservations and information about the lake and camping.

Directions: From the town of Demopolis, go 3 miles east on U.S. Highway 80. Turn left on County Road 43 at the signs directing you to the lake and go about 2 miles to the park entrance.

For more information: Alabama Wildlife and Freshwater Fisheries Division; U.S. Army Corps of Engineers.

29 Gainesville Lake

Key species: Largemouth bass, crappie, catfish, hybrid striped bass, bream.

Overview: Impounded in 1978, Gainesville Lake has become very well-known for its excellent largemouth bass fishery. Created by the Howell Heflin Lock and Dam on the Tombigbee River, Gainesville Lake covers almost 6,500 acres. The lake was created for navigation and flood control, but the fine fishing has become a very important side benefit.

Description: There are eight public use areas with convenient banks access and boat ramps on the reservoir. Located in western Alabama, the lake is midway between

Gainesville has a strong population of big catfish.

One down and more to go this morning.

Tuscaloosa, and Meridian, Mississippi. The Gainesville Lock and the dam spillway have launch ramps with plenty of good parking. Below the dam in the tailrace waters, good hybrid bass and catfish are commonly encountered. Studies show that large numbers of 18-inch bass are present, but even larger fish have been caught.

The fishing: As in most of the dammed river lakes, Gainesville's best fishing is off the main body of the lake. Bass anglers should work submerged cover such as trees, dock pilings, and weed beds. Buzz baits and large spinner baits are good for bass. Early and late, top-water baits can be good bets for larger bass. Crappie anglers should work deeper creek channels in the lake. Live minnow and small light-colored jigs work well on the specks. For bream, anglers should focus on weed growth in sloughs and other shallow water areas.

Delorme: Alabama Atlas & Gazetteer: Page 34 C3.

Camping: The Cochrane Recreation Area has overnight camping with sixty camp-sites. S.W. Taylor Park has twenty-three picnic sites, but no camping is allowed.

Tips and cautions: Gainesville Lake is a good destination for bank anglers. A wide range of docks, piers, and cleared shoreline make fishing from the bank easier here than in many lakes.

Directions: From Tuscaloosa, take Interstate 59 southwest. Take the Gainesville exit, going north on Highway 39. From Gainesville take Highway 116 west and then take County Road 85 north. On CR 85 signs are posted giving directions to the dam site and the lake access points.

For more information: Alabama Wildlife and Freshwater Fisheries Division.

30 Holt Reservoir

Key species: Largemouth bass, spotted bass, crappie, bream.

Overview: Holt Reservoir is on the Black Warrior River just north of Tuscaloosa. Built in 1965, the lake is not large for a Corps of Engineers lake, with only 3,300 acres in coverage, but because of its proximity to Tuscaloosa, it gets quite a bit of traffic and recreational boater use. There are seven parks along the 18-mile long lake.

Crawfish baits attract Holt bass.

Description: The primary uses of Holt Reservoir are navigation, flood control, and recreation; fishing is prominent in the recreational use. Bald eagles visit Holt in winter (as they do a number of lakes in Alabama). Fishing in the lake's upper headwaters as they exit Bankhead Dam is quite popular since the moving water provides good fishing for catfish, striped bass, largemouth bass, and spotted bass.

The fishing: Holt Reservoir has its ups and downs as far as fishing goes. Some years are quite good, and the next year may not be as good. Probably the relatively small size of the lake accounts for this variation. Generally, the bass fishing is quite reliably good. Largemouth are more commonly caught in the backwaters by anglers using spinner baits, slow-working plastics near cover, and sometimes on top-water baits such as stickbaits, which can be "walked" across the surface. Spotted bass are more often found in deeper areas of the lake where they hit shad imitating plugs such as Hotspots and silver-colored spinner baits. A very good bream fishery is found in Holt. Anglers looking for big bream should focus on the sloughs and shallow flats near cover. Live bait is best.

DeLorme: Alabama Atlas & Gazetteer: Page 29 H9.

Camping: Deerlick Creek Park provides camping on the lake. It has forty modern sites and six primitive camping sites. Boat ramps and recreation areas are located at the park, also.

Tips and cautions: The Corps of Engineers has constructed a number of substantial fish attraction structures near Deerlick Park. They are marked with red-and-white buoys.

Directions: From Tuscaloosa, take Highway 216 about 6 miles to the dam site area.

For more information: Alabama Wildlife and Freshwater Fisheries Division; U.S. Army Corps of Engineers.

31 Aliceville Lake

Key species: Largemouth bass, crappie, catfish in the tailwaters below the dam, bream.

Overview: A fairly recent lake, built in 1980 by the Corps of Engineers, Aliceville is nearly 8,500 acres in coverage. Aliceville is popular with anglers in both Alabama and Mississippi since it straddles the border between the two states.

Description: Aliceville's largemouth bass represent its most popular fishery. Bass do very well in this lake, and large numbers of three- to four-pound bass are present. Crappie likewise are in very good shape here, with a 9-inch minimum size restriction. There are a number of lake access points, and since it is only 12 miles north of Aliceville, it is easy to get to.

The fishing: Top-water fishing is quite popular at Aliceville Lake. Bass respond to old favorite top-waters such as Devil's Horse, Jitterbugs, and large bladed buzz baits worked in and around heavy cover. Of course, bass always can be caught on large plastic worms worked around deeper cover. Crappie can be found most of the warmer parts of the year around deep cover: trees, fallen limbs, and under docks. Small jigs worked very slowly and live minnows are traditional favorites. During the spring, the crappie move into spawning territory; shallow flats with vegetation overhead are good. Anglers work the backwaters such as sloughs and smaller creeks with live baits for bream, which can be very large. Many local anglers use heavy gear and large live baits below Tom Bevill Lock and Dam for catfish. Be prepared to lose some tackle if you go tailrace fish, but you can also expect to hook into some big ones, too.

DeLorme: *Alabama Atlas & Gazetteer:* Page 34 A3.

Camping: There are day-use facilities at Pickensville Park, and the primary camp-ground is at Pickensville Campground. There are about 180 campsites, two launch ramps, docks, and cleaning stations.

Tips and cautions: As on any of the navigation lakes, anglers must exercise caution around commercial barge traffic and around the lock and dam.

Directions: From Tuscaloosa, take Interstate 20/Interstate 59 southwest. Take the exit for Highway 14. Follow Highway 14 through Aliceville. The lake is just 1 mile past Pickensville and Tom Bevill Lock and Dam, right off Highway 14.

Big Aliceville bream respond to live bait.

For more information: Alabama Wildlife and Freshwater Fisheries Division; U.S. Army Corps of Engineers.

32 Lake Lurleen

Key species: Bream, catfish, crappie, largemouth bass.

Overview: This small 250-acre lake is situated within Lake Lurleen State Park, which is 9 miles northwest of Tuscaloosa. Boat launching is available on the lake.

Description: Although Lake Lurleen is small by Alabama standards, its intimate size doesn't mean that it isn't worth the trouble. Indeed, small lakes such as this are perfect for introducing small children and grandchildren to the pleasures of fishing. Park facilities include a campground, picnic area, and pavilions. Fishing piers and swimming areas are available. This is great place to take kids to get them started on their fishing education. A cane pole or spin-cast rig with live bait would get nearly any kid interested in fishing.

Being located near the University of Alabama, many nonfishing activities are possible. Lake Lurleen State Park hosts two annual major events: the Annual Youth Fishing Tournament and the Lake Lurleen Triathlon.

Big yellow-belly bream provide great sport and good eating.

The fishing: Some very good catfish are taken in Lake Lurleen as well as good stringers of bream and crappie. Live bait is best; worms will take both catfish and bream as will crickets. For catfish, try two or three rods baited with different live baits, such as worms, minnows, and catalpa worms, to try to establish a pattern of what the fish want on any particular day. Some days it doesn't matter: They'll eat everything. Other days, the catfish can be very picky.

Small minnows are the ticket for the crappie. In the spring, especially April, the crappie go up into the shallows especially under limbs and near stuff in the water to spawn, and they are easy to catch. A minnow under a bobber set at about 3 feet would be a good starting technique.

For bass — and there are some quite respectable largemouth in Lake Lurleen — try plastic worms and spinner baits around structure and indentions in the bank. When there is lots of activity on the lake such as during the summer weekends, probably the best idea would be to fish the lake at night. Dark top-water lures can be effective when worked slowly down a bank. Try to give the darkness-feeding bass plenty of time and opportunity to locate and home in on the bait. Lake Lurleen is a very good bank fishing lake, but boats are allowed. Because of its rather small size, boats such as canoes and small flat-bottomed boats would probably be best.

DeLorme: Alabama Atlas & Gazetteer: Page 29 H7.

Camping: A very nice campground is on-site.

Tips and cautions: Overnight camping charges at the park range from $17.50 to $19.00 per night depending on services used. A word of caution: During the football season, when 'Bama is playing at home, don't even think of trying to get a place to camp at Lake Lurleen. Fans reserve these spaces a long time in advance.

Directions: From Tuscaloosa, take Interstate 359/Highway 69. At the intersection with U.S. Highway 82, take a left onto US 82 going west. Turn right onto County Road 21. Follow the signs to park.

For more information: Alabama Wildlife and Freshwater Fisheries Division; Lake Lurleen State Park.

Birmingham Region

You know, it must surely say something about fishing in Alabama when in the immediate area of the state's capital and largest city, some absolutely gorgeous and productive fishing waters exist. Big cities and good fishing are not usually associated, but this is Alabama, and we do things our own way.

In this region are some very pretty lakes that are full of gamefish. Smith Lake, in particular, has clear, clean water, and some of the largest spotted bass to be found anywhere. Also, this region has Alabama's only full-time public trout stream.

If this isn't enough, some of the finest warm-water floating and wading streams to be found anywhere run through this part of Alabama. If you are a float-trip angler, then the Cahaba and Locust Fork Rivers should be on your list of "must-do" streams.

Since the big city of Birmingham lies in this area, visiting anglers will have no trouble finding supplies, equipment, food, lodging, and advice from stores and shops in the area. However, rather than the "stuff" that is here, most anglers will enjoy the "place" of the Birmingham area more. The pleasure provided by this region just increases when a big spotted bass or striper starts going the other way when hooked.

33 Cahaba River

Key species: Largemouth bass, spotted bass, bluegill and other sunfish, crappie, chain pickerel, catfish.

Overview: The Cahaba River has a watershed of about 1,900 miles, and it flows through central Alabama, including the Birmingham area.

Description: This is the longest free-flowing river in the state, and it moves from relatively unspoiled, unpopulated areas in its upper reaches to the hustle and bustle near Birmingham. As the river leaves the immediate Birmingham area, the number of people using the river drops off again, and the fishing gets even better. All along its length, different groups of enthusiasts use the river for different purposes. Near its beginnings, kayakers, canoeists, and waders enjoy the beautiful and endangered plants and animal life. As the river nears the heavier populated areas, johnboats and other craft become more popular. One thing is certain, all along its length the fishing can be quite good.

Recent growth of the metropolitan Birmingham area has somewhat degraded the water quality of the lower parts of the river, but it is still a gem. The Cahaba has more visitors (anglers, floaters, swimmers) than any other free-flowing river in the state. The Cahaba, because of its high population of location-specific species, has been proposed for National Wild and Scenic River status.

The fishing: This is a good float stream, and for anglers who enjoy this quality form of fishing, it is hard to beat. Largemouth and two kinds of spotted bass are present, and fishing near rocks, blown-down trees, and other structure is a good way to catch bass. A very wide range of sunfish and other panfish are present. In the deeper holes, catfish hold toward the bottom structure. The Cahaba is a prime fly rod and light spinning rod stream. Keep in mind that the overall size of bass and other gamefish caught here will be smaller than in the larger Alabama lakes and rivers. However, most anglers who fish here think that a three-pound bass caught in the Cahaba is just as good a catch as an eight-pounder caught in the larger bodies of water.

For both bass and panfish, crankbaits and jigs in smaller sizes (one-thirty-second- to one-eighth ounce weight) are very effective. Soft plastics such as worms, jigs, and tube lures are very productive, and they tend to not get hung up quite as often as hard plastic lures or metal lures. No matter what sort of artificial is used, it should resemble a crawfish. Worked slowly around rocks, boulders, and other bottom structure, crawfish imitations are deadly. Of course, a live crawfish on an unweighted hook allowed to drift around the bottom structure is probably the most effective of all possible baits.

It must be noted that the Cahaba usually has a fairly high traffic flow of boaters, and this can disrupt fishing at times. Please be polite and patient when other

Cahaba River largemouth bass often take spinners.

Birmingham Region

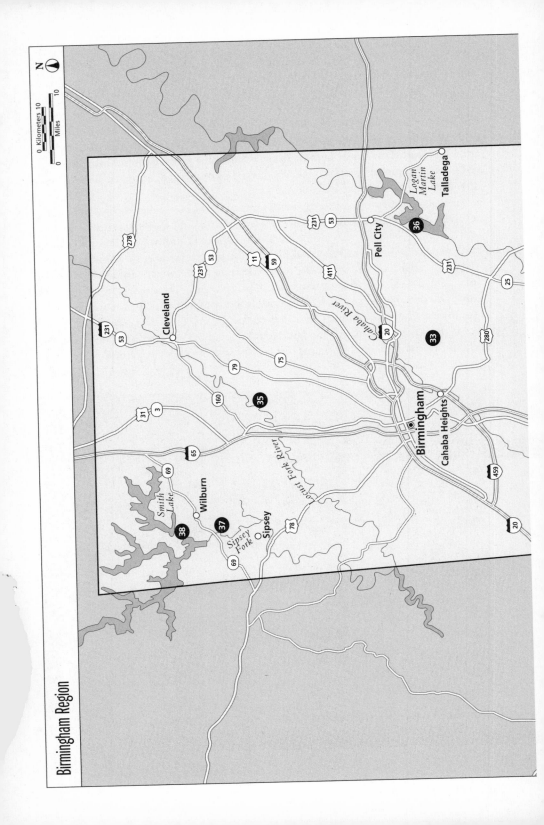

Birmingham Region

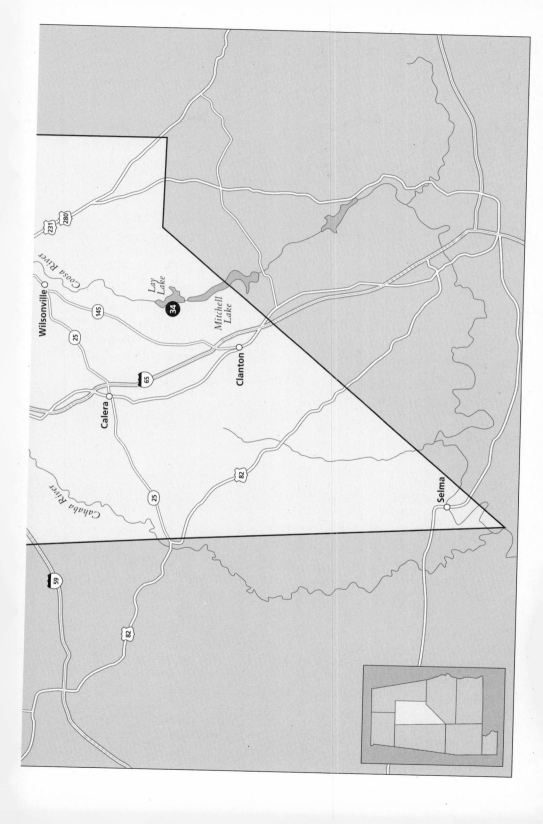

users come through, even if they mess up the hole you're fishing for a little while. A good idea to cut down on the disruption factor is to plan an overnight camping float so that you can fish very early and late when other boaters are not using the water. Unless very heavy rains occur, this can be the very best way to experience the Cahaba and its angling.

DeLorme: Alabama Atlas & Gazetteer: Page 31 C8, D7, E7, F7.

Camping and lodging: For those who prefer a civilized night's sleep, there are many motels in the Birmingham area. However, Cahaba floaters have streamside access, and overnight camping trips on the river are permitted. Have a good, lightweight tent for rainy or buggy nights.

Tips and cautions: If an angler is lucky enough to fish the Cahaba when the Cahaba lilies are in bloom, he or she is in for a special treat. These are gorgeous water plants.

Alabama Small Boats in Helena can provide rental boats or shuttle service for float anglers.

Directions: This will vary depending upon the part of the river to be fished. A good plan is to take Interstate 459 east off Interstate 65 south of Birmingham. I-459 runs roughly parallel to the river for several miles, and can provide access. Lower reaches of the stream can be accessed by contacting Alabama Small Boats in Helena.

For more information: Alabama Wildlife and Freshwater Fisheries Division; Cahaba River Society (www.cahabariversociety.org).

34 Lay Lake

Key species: Largemouth and spotted bass, crappie, bream, striped bass.

Overview: Only thirty-five minutes south of Birmingham, Lay Lake is a hydro-electric generating facility that also offers very good recreation possibilities for Birmingham residents. Lay Lake was created in 1914 when the Coosa River was dammed.

Description: Seven public access areas give anglers multiple choices of launch sites. The upper end of Lay Lake, the tailwaters of Logan Martin Dam, is very heavily fished during spring runs of hybrid stripers. When shad run upstream, largemouth and spotted bass fishing is very popular with area anglers. Bass Masters Classic Tournaments have been held on Lay Lake because of its relatively high populations of 18-inch and larger bass. In fact, bass tournaments are held on Lay Lake quite often. Despite its high level of use, Lay Lake is a good place to catch some fine fish.

Being so close to both Birmingham and Montgomery, Lay Lake gets a great deal of water sport activities during most summer days.

The fishing: Both largemouth and spotted bass respond well to shad-imitation

Another top-water bass makes for a great day at Lay Lake.

crankbaits, tube baits, and spinner baits. In the spring and summer, anglers should work shallow, weedy flats. Big fish are sometimes caught in very thin water when they are just on or just off their spawning beds. When a promising creek or cove is found, a larger top-water such as a chugger or popper can bring strong strikes. Don't get in a hurry, and don't overwork the bait. Let it sit while the water quiets down. During the summer, anglers may have to resort to night fishing for bass if the daytime commotion gets too loud and disruptive. Keep in mind that there are some very big fish in Lay Lake, and they don't get big by being dumb. Keep working, and they will respond.

Crappie are quite common, especially in deeper, wooded parts of the lake. Live minnows and small tube jigs in bright colors are effective on Lay Lake crappie. During the spring crappie will be thick in 3- to 4-foot water, especially where overhanging limbs or fallen timber is in the water.

Bream are very thick during warmer months, especially up feeder creek channels around vegetation. Anglers serious about fishing Lay Lake should pay a great deal of attention to creek channels and shallow backwaters. During the spring, some coves and backwaters get absolutely full of bedding bream. The best way to collect the main ingredient of a fish fry is to cast a lightly weighted worm under a small bobber into these quiet shallows.

White bass and stripers will more likely be found around deeper, main lake river channels. There is a very good spring fishery for white bass, hybrid stripers, and stripers in the upstream waters of Lay Lake. Anglers should work the tailwaters of Logan Martin Dam as water is released in the spring since all of these fish run as far upstream as possible before spawning. Silver and chrome spoons that can be cast long distances and sink fairly fast are good.

DeLorme: Alabama Atlas & Gazetteer: Page 38 B1.

Camping and lodging: Lodging is available at the lake at the Alabama 4-H Center. It offers a wide range of visitor housing from large conventions to individual anglers.

Tips and cautions: There is a fish consumption advisory for fish caught in Lay Lake due to the presence of PCBs in tested fish.

Guide service is available through Sunrise Anglers, which specializes in fly fishing, (205) 669-2110, and Reeds Guide Service, (205) 787-5133.

Directions: Easy navigation. From Birmingham, take Interstate 65 south. At Calera take Highway 25 east to Wilsonville. At Wilsonville take County Road 61/ Highway 145 south. The road runs alongside Lay Lake.

For more information: Alabama Wildlife and Freshwater Fisheries Division; Lay Lake Home Owners and Boat Owners Association, P.O. Box 354, Wilsonville, AL 35186.

35 Locust Fork River

Key species: Spotted bass, largemouth bass, various bream, catfish.

Overview: How a river so fine can be located so close to the largest metropolitan area in the state is a mystery, but it is a fact. Birmingham is very close, but as of yet the potential harmful effects of big-city run-off pollution have not had a negative impact on this wonderful river.

Description: The Locust Fork is primarily a float fishing stream in its lower reaches, below the Highway 160 Bridge. From this point until the stream joins the Black Warrior, it is usually fishable for most float anglers. It is still actively moving, but not to the point that anglers spend more time paddling and praying than fishing. Above this point, it is a very challenging whitewater stream that is probably too active for most anglers. For those who are determined to fish the middle reaches above the Swann Covered Bridge, walk in and wade fishing might be the best idea.

Streamside vegetation and wildlife is outstanding. Especially in the spring, anglers and floaters will be rewarded with lots of flowers and blooming trees as the stream floats you down. At all times, anglers and floaters will be impressed by the massive rock bluffs and cliffs that continually renew themselves as the river runs toward its meeting with the other Black Warrior River forks. This is a spectacular place, but it may not be for everyone who fishes. It will take some effort to get to the Locust Fork, and it will require some reaction to changing water flow and conditions. However, it is so outstanding in its scenery and wildness that many anglers will find it irresistible.

North Alabama has some fantastic creeks for light-tackle fishing.

Even with the damages caused by being so close to urban sprawl, Locust Fork is a treasure of huge proportions. The National Park Service has placed the Locust Fork in the top 2 percent of all U.S. rivers. The Locust Fork is the major tributary of the Black Warrior River and is the second longest free-flowing river in the state. Fantastic geologic formations and some outstanding whitewater rapids make the Locust Fork a very popular destination for kayakers and canoeists. The river itself is subject to rainfall effects, and can range from low-water, almost dry conditions to raging-out-of-its-banks flood conditions. Anglers and floaters must be aware of this at all times.

The fishing: Once an angler finds himself or herself on the Locust Fork, how to fish it becomes easier. It all looks fishy, but some places are just better. Look for large underwater boulders and other stone structure. Fish will be there. Largemouth and spotted bass will be pretty well mixed together in the general river run, but most anglers will catch more spots than largemouth. Some of the bass in Locust Fork will run five pounds, but the general run of bass is about two pounds. Good bets are small (4 inches or less) dark-colored plastic worms. Dark-colored jigs are good, too. These baits no doubt resemble hellgrammites, which are prime bass food. Crawfish-colored and patterned baits can be quite productive. Sometimes smaller swimming-type top-water lures cast near shoreline structure such as downed trees and boulders can be lots of fun.

Crawfish imitations cast near rocks will yield Locust Fork bass.

For the bream, everything that goes for bass goes for them. The only difference is that the baits need to be a bit smaller. Instead of plastic worms, perhaps a tube jig might work better for bream. There are some very big bluegill in the Locust Fork, and they will hit at nearly anything that passes them by.

Finally, probably the most fun possible on the Locust Fork would be the long rod. Fly fishing a small, dark-colored popping bug might be a whole lot of fun. Both the bream and many of the bass would be more than happy to knock a bug into the air a little bit. A fly rod and its line would be a complication when the angler has to run the boat down a shoal, but it would sure be a kick in the fishing water!

DeLorme: Alabama Atlas & Gazetteer: Page 25 F7.

Camping and lodging: None close. Probably the best bet for anglers would be to stay in an area motel on Interstate 65 and drive to the put-in/take-out points.

Tips and cautions: As with all hill-country streams, anglers must be aware of rapidly rising water, particularly after heavy rains upstream.

Directions: Somewhat difficult. From I-65 north of Birmingham take exit 284 to Highway 160. Go east on Highway 160 toward Cleveland. Before Cleveland, Highway 160 will cross Locust Fork. This is a good place to start a float/wade trip.

For more information: Alabama Wildlife and Freshwater Fisheries Division.

36 Logan Martin Lake

Key species: Largemouth bass, spotted bass, striped bass, hybrid striped bass, crappie.

Overview: Another one of the fabulous Coosa River impoundments, Logan Martin Lake covers 15,300 acres and gives anglers in the Birmingham area access to some fine fishing. The lake extends from its dam site nearly 50 miles to the tailwaters of Neely Henry Dam, where some very good fishing can be had during spring spawning runs.

These Logan Martin bass were caught on a jig and pig combo.

Description: A number of good access areas are used by anglers on Logan Martin Lake, and there at least three free public boat ramps. There is considerable shoreline development in places, and boat docks have become a popular form of artificial structure for bass anglers. Because of its proximity to Birmingham, Logan Martin Lake receives a great deal of recreational boating activity during the daylight hours. Sometimes this forces anglers to concentrate their efforts on night fishing or very early morning fishing.

The fishing: Bass fishing can be outstanding on Logan Martin Lake, and both spotted bass and largemouth grow fast and get pretty big here. In fact, studies have shown the bass in Logan Martin tend to be the best conditioned and healthiest fish in the state. As in most of the Coosa River lakes, spotted bass are thick in number

We're having catfish for supper!

and respond well to shad imitations fished around deep, open-water type structure. Steep banks and large rocks are good places to try a spinner bait or crankbait in silver and chrome finishes. Largemouth bass tend to hide out in backwaters and sloughs, and if a shallow creek channel or point with weed cover or fallen timber can be found, it deserves attention with weedless plastic baits. Big, dark plastic worms fished slowly on the bottom in old creek channels can yield some very good largemouth bass.

There is a great white bass, hybrid striper, and striper fishery in Logan Martin, especially in the spring when these fish run upstream all the way to Neely Henry Dam. Anglers can really load up with some fun fish when the current is running strong from the dam. Caution must be exercised: There are lots of rocks and other obstructions, and fast water can make them a challenge. These spring-run fish tend to find spoons, spinners, and live bait such as shad and big minnows very attractive. Very good striper and hybrid fishing can be found on both Ohatchee and Choccollocco Creeks. Each spring season is different, and if fewer fish than usual migrate down from Weiss Lake, the striper and white bass fishing may not be as strong as other years.

Crappie fishing is a strong point of the Logan Martin offerings. A very good hatch of crappie in 2004 and good survival since then has loaded the lake with some very big speckled perch. Traditional techniques and timing work here. Live minnows fished below a bobber around shoreline cover and small light-colored jigs, either feather or soft plastic, work very well. A very good option for rapid crappie action is to combine the two best bait choices; a one-eighth ounce jig tipped with a live minnow hooked through the lips and cast to shallow water cover is a good way to load up on slabs.

DeLorme: Alabama Atlas & Gazetteer: Page 32 E1, D2.

Camping: Some very well-equipped and popular private marinas and campgrounds are found on Logan Martin Lake. Lakeside Landing Marina (205-525-5701) is recommended.

Tips and cautions: Anglers should be aware that fish consumption advisories on Logan Martin Lake and Choccollocco Creek are in place due to PCBs found in fish.

Directions: From Birmingham, go east on Interstate 20. Follow direction signs from Pell City.

For more information: Alabama Wildlife and Freshwater Fisheries Division.

37 Sipsey Fork

Key species: Rainbow trout, striped bass, hybrid bass, white bass, skipjack herring.

Overview: When the water leaves Smith Lake, it is something that is very rare for Alabama water: COLD! No matter the season, the water that exits deep and clear

Smith Lake is too chilly for most native fish species. This doesn't mean that Sipsey Fork is fishless, however. There are many brilliantly colored and hard-fighting fish here: rainbow trout.

Description: This is not a "captive" fishing situation for trout and trout anglers. The trout portion of the river extends 50 miles downstream from the Smith Dam site, so anglers and trout have a lot of territory to wander around in. Trout are stocked, usually every sixty days or so, by the state and in cooperation with the U.S. Fish and Wildlife Service. Most of the stockers are 8- to 10-inch fish, but sometimes larger fish are released. Brandon Johnson, who runs Riverside Outfitters and Fly Shop, which is right at the Highway 69 crossing of Sipsey Fork, tells me that five-pounders are caught every year, so the fish do survive and do prosper here. The fish are released at the dam site, and after release they quickly work their way downstream for several miles.

Since Smith Lake and Sipsey Fork are so close to Birmingham, quite a few anglers take advantage of the unique fishery, and visitors from all over the world come here to try their luck on trout. The water is clear and cold, and anglers who usually wade fish Alabama's creeks and streams in cut-offs may want to invest in some good insulated waders; the water gets colder the higher above the knees it gets. A word of caution here: Anglers should be careful when walking down the trails to get to the river. The banks of Sipsey Fork tend to be either rock or a very slippery form of mud. Watch your step! A wrong step on that slick mud and you may find yourself bouncing down the bank. I have had this happen, and it is not fun.

This would be a wonderful stream to float in a canoe or kayak for fishing; take it slowly and work the deeper pools and pockets with a riffle at the head. There is a good access road just before the Highway 69 Bridge, which will take anglers alongside the stream for a couple of miles upstream to the Water Pumping Station, which is a good place to start fishing. There are pull-offs on this road at several places that provide walking paths to the river.

The Sipsey Fork is subject to power generation at the dam, and water levels can fluctuate greatly in a short period of time. If you are fishing and you hear a loud tornado warning type siren, start heading to the bank; some water is coming.

The fishing: The brightly colored rainbow trout get most of the attention in Sipsey Fork, but they are not the only fish worth working for. In the spring during their spawning runs, striped bass, hybrid bass, and white bass all congregate in huge numbers below Smith Dam, and the action can be absolutely incredible. These are not just little fish, either. Some very large stripers and hybrids gather here. The Alabama record hybrid striper came from below Smith Dam. When these big bruisers are on the prowl, any bait that looks like a shad will work. Silver spoons and white jigs, either bucktail or soft plastic grubs, will work well. How fast to work the shad look-alike? Some days they want them worked slowly near the bottom. Other days, the bait must be ripping through the water. Anglers must experiment to find what the fish want on any particular day.

A unique fishery for skipjack herring occurs during the spring, also. These fish also swim upstream to spawn, and they have to stop at Smith Dam. At this time, the

This youngster has the Sipsey Fork trout figured out.

skipjacks will hit nearly anything that is moving quickly; speed is the ticket. Bright lures such as spoons, spinners, and light-colored jigs are all good, but they must be whipped through the water to attract the herring's attention. The skipjacks are great fighters and very good jumpers, but most folks don't care for them as table fare: too oily and bony. Most of the herring are released after capture.

Now, for the star attraction of the Sipsey Fork show: rainbow trout. Alabama is way out of the fish's normal range, but because of the very cold and well-oxygenated water that comes from the bottom of Smith Lake through the dam, rainbows do very well here. The only change most Alabama anglers will have to make when fishing the Sipsey Fork rainbows is to tackle down. This is not the place for twenty-pound lines and level-wind reels. Four- to six-pound line on an ultra-light spinning rig is good. Rooster tails and Mepps spinners are all good hardware baits for rainbow trout. Even very small Rapalas, about 2 inches or so, work well. However, for real results, nothing beats live bait. Crickets on small gold hooks about 18 inches below small split shot are great. Cast upstream and let the current move the bait downstream as the bait sinks. Watch the line! Often the bite will be indicated with just a twitch of the line as the trout bumps the bait. For day-in/day-out best results, good old redworms are a good bet. Thread a good healthy worm on a small gold hook with splitshot. Throw it upstream above a deeper hole of water, and hold on. If a trout is there, it will at least taste the worm. Some very good results for the trout come by using Berkeley PowerBait and Berkeley Power-eggs. The bright chartreuse color seems to be best. A good place to start looking for Sipsey Fork rainbows is at the Pumping

Station, which is at the end of the dirt road that runs to the right of the river before Highway 69 crosses the big bridge over the river. Good parking is there, and a path leads to a good, deep hole where trout like to group up and feed.

Many anglers come here to fly fish for rainbows. There are natural insect hatches on the Sipsey Fork, but most of the emergent insect life is small, so fly anglers have to match the hatch with small midge-type flies; below the surface flies are probably best. Brandon Johnson, of Riverside Fly Shop, tells me that there are daily midge hatches on the river, and the trout will respond well to midge imitations in small (#18 is about as big as possible) midge flies. Preferred fly colors and midge patterns seem to change every day. Most fly anglers use five-weight or smaller rods. A very good place to get equipment, specific flies and lures, and good advice and information is Riverside Outfitter and Fly Shop (256-287-9582), which is located 4 miles below Smith Dam. Guide service is available there.

Unlike most other states that have trout fishing areas, Alabama does not require anglers to have additional trout stamps or licenses. Just the regular Alabama fishing license entitles anglers to fish for trout and catch and keep the daily five-trout limit.

DeLorme: Alabama Atlas & Gazetteer: Page 24 G2, G3.

Camping and lodging: None close. Probably the best camping bet would be one of the Smith Lake campgrounds. There are motels at both the Interstate 65 exit and at Jasper.

Tips and cautions: Anglers must be very careful when fishing Sipsey Fork. Water levels can rise very quickly with little or no warning. Before wading out to a great-looking spot, make sure you have a return path already picked out.

Directions: Easy. From Birmingham take I-65 north to exit 299. Go west on Highway 69 past Wilburn. Turn right onto County Road 43; the dam site will be about 5 miles ahead, but there are good pull-offs along the way.

For more information: Alabama Wildlife and Freshwater Fisheries Division.

38 Smith Lake

Key species: Spotted bass, striped bass, largemouth bass, crappie, various bream.

Overview: Smith Lake is a very deep and clear lake occupying parts of Cullman, Walker, and Winston Counties northeast of Birmingham. The lake was created in 1961 by Alabama Power Company, which constructed the Lewis Smith Dam on the Sipsey Fork of the Black Warrior River.

Description: The lake has three main branches: the Sipsey Fork, Rock Creek, and Ryan Creek. Sections of Smith Lake occupy part of Bankhead National Forest, and have three National Forest Recreation areas: Corinth, Clear Creek, and Houston. There is considerable shoreline development on parts of the shoreline. At most highway crossings, development seems to be booming with marinas, condos, and other big buildings going up. Anglers may have to work a number of points to locate fish and establish a pattern. The lake offers a wide range of structure and bottom types, but typically the shoreline features very steep banks and abrupt drop-offs. The bottom is typically rocky with either massive boulders or smaller chunk-type rocks. There are also many feeder streams, all of which can be very productive at different times. Gamefish tend to relocate often in Smith Lake, and this can make finding them quite difficult. As mentioned earlier, Smith Lake tends to be very clear, and anglers used to fishing waters with more color and less visibility may need to lighten up on line weight. Smith Lake deserves every angler's attention; it's a special place.

Smith Dam is not very wide, but it is very high. Over 500 miles of shoreline exist on the lake. Although Smith Lake is not the largest lake in Alabama at only 21,000 acres, because of its great depth, it may hold more water than any other lake in the state.

The fishing: There is much to say about the fishing on Smith Lake, and most of it is very good. Just about the only negative aspect of fishing Smith Lake is that it requires anglers to adjust their thinking to fit the lake's deep and clear water. The

This fine Smith Lake bass was caught on a spinner.

heavy lines and rigs that work well on Weiss and Guntersville may be too visible for the bass here. Bass in particular tend to move around a lot in Smith Lake, and this makes finding and keeping a pattern tough. However, the quality of fish in this deep old lake makes the extra effort worth it.

Let's look at spotted bass first. How about producing the state record spotted bass: an 8-pound 15-ounce giant caught in 1978? That is an outstanding spotted bass anywhere in the world. Spots are usually caught on crawfish imitations. Jigs and pigs, tube lures, and deep running crankbaits in crawfish colors are all good here. The key is to get the lures down to the fish and near structure. Rocks, ledges, rock piles, creek edges—these are places where Smith Lake's spots tend to gather. Good places to start a search for a record spotted bass are Dismal Creek, where the current record came from; Brushy Creek; and Rock Creek.

Largemouth bass are present in good numbers in Smith Lake, and an angler using gear for spotted bass is just about as likely to come across a nice largemouth bass, too. Generally, the largemouth are found farther back in the creek arms and in shallower water. However, both largemouth and spots eat the same food and like the same sort of structure, so they often are found grouped up together. Some very good top-water action occurs early and late up the larger creek arms. Walk the Dog – type stick baits are lots of fun when the bass are chasing shad in shallow water.

Now, let's look at the big boys, striped bass. The state record, a 32-pound, 8-ounce crusher, came from Smith Lake. These are Gulf Coast strain stripers, and even though there is no indication that the fish have ever reproduced, enough have been stocked by the state to ensure a good population of line-sided monsters. Remember, they run in schools, so catching a solo is rare. Anglers looking for one of these trophies need to concentrate on deep drop-offs near the main lake body. A good accurate fish finder is very important. Look for the big schools of shad, and the stripers won't be far away. The very best bet for bait is to send a live shad down to the level of the fish indicated on the screen; use just enough weight to take the poor shad down, not too much. Live shad are usually obtained at the dam site by netting and at other marinas. For artificial baits, anglers like to use shad look-alike crankbaits and other swimming plugs. Sometimes these must be rigged with weights to get them to the depth of the stripers. Slow trolling with deep running silver-finished lures can be very good. Captain Bill Vines, a Smith Lake guide with Stripe Fishing Headquarters (205-647-7683), tells me that the best months for large stripers are March, April, and May. The best areas of the lake during these months will be up the three main creek arms. As the season moves on to summer, anglers should focus their attention closer to the dam site and deeper water. Captain Bill says that artificials used for stripers on Smith Lake should have at least a flash of white somewhere on the lure. Fly anglers even get in on the striper action when the fish are on top chasing shad. Some very big stripers have been caught on fly rods here.

Crappie are very good in Smith Lake during the spring spawn. Anglers fishing up creeks and in whatever timber and shoreline structure can be found often catch heavy strings of slabs. Small jigs and live minnows are the best bet. Later in the summer, crappie tend to disperse and loosely school near deep-water structure such as old trees and fallen brush.

There are good ramps and marinas at several locations on the lake. Some very good and free ramps are at the dam site. Lots of parking, and ramps face different directions to make sandy day launches easier.

DeLorme: Alabama Atlas & Gazetteer: Page 24 G2, E4.

Camping: Excellent facilities are available at Smith Lake Park near Trimble. Camper hookups and tent camping sites are there along with a good boat ramp and other facilities. Information on the camping can be obtained at (256) 739-2916.

Tips and cautions: Anglers should be aware that catching and keeping bass in the 13- to 15-inch range is not allowed. Fish over this size and especially under this size are legal. Harvesting bass under 13 inches is encouraged in order to keep smaller bass from overpopulating the lake—and these are some good eating fish!

Directions: From Birmingham, take Interstate 65 north. Take the Highway 69 exit. Go west on Highway 69 until it reaches the lake near Powellville.

For more information: Alabama Wildlife and Freshwater Fisheries Division; Alabama Power Company.

Northeast Region

Anglers in northeast Alabama have some wonderful choices to make. Freshwater game species in great abundance offer anglers a wide range of fishing methods and opportunities.

In the big lakes, some of the world's finest largemouth bass fishing exists. This is bass boat heaven. Lake Guntersville in particular is just a fantastic place to seek big largemouth bass. While Guntersville is probably the region's premier attraction, it is not the only game in town. Lake Weiss and all of the other region's lakes demand attention. All of the major lakes in the northeast have fine ramps and storage facilities.

Small-water fishing in the northeast region is great. Personally, I am very partial to fishing creeks and streams, and some of the most beautiful small water I've ever seen, and I've been lucky enough to fish in some world-class fishing locations, flows in the northeast region of Alabama. These small streams may require a little walk in and out, but most are not a major undertaking to get on. Anglers fishing the creeks and streams should think about downsizing their tackle, line, and lures. The fish aren't as big as in the major lakes, but they pull just as hard, and the beauty of the water they occupy makes the smaller size of the fish no big deal.

So let's take a look at the northeast region of Alabama: It's a great place to wet a line!

39 Lake Guntersville

Key species: Largemouth bass, spotted bass, striped bass, hybrid bass, crappie, bream, catfish.

Overview: Guntersville is a huge lake. It stretches for 75 miles from its upper reaches at Nickajack Dam to Guntersville Dam at the lower end, and it has a surface area of nearly 70,000 acres. It is a massive body of water that was formed when the Tennessee River was dammed by the Tennessee Valley Authority (TVA) in order to generate electricity and control periodic flooding.

Description: Guntersville is too big to be easily or quickly summarized. An angler could visit a different part of the lake every week and still never get the lake completely covered. Some good advice for visiting anglers would be to pick a section of the lake, fish it hard, and try to learn how to work that area. Trying to cover the entire lake in just a single trip is impossible. However, most resident anglers see the lake as being best divided into upper and lower sections. In the middle region, about Scottsboro, the lake can be logically placed into an upper, more riverlike section, and into a lower, more typically lake section. Except for the main river channels, Guntersville is basically a backwater, shallow flats lake. The big difference between

Bass bite well in early spring on Guntersville.

Guntersville and other similar lakes is its size. Guntersville gives anglers mile upon mile of very bass-friendly water with thick milfoil grass beds and stump fields.

In addition to its obvious economic benefits, the creation of Lake Guntersville also created one of the premier big bass lakes in the world. Along the shores of Guntersville, various marinas, residential development, and municipal facilities give visiting anglers a very wide range of eating and overnighting choices. Many boat launch facilities are available to anglers from the dam site area all the way up both shores of the lake. However, only in a very few places does the lake seem overly developed. There are still many miles of wild and unspoiled shorelines. For those anglers with nonfishing family members, the surrounding towns have a wide range of arts and crafts and other entertainment options. There are some world-class parks and recreational facilities on the shores of Guntersville. Many, many bass tournaments are held every year at Lake Guntersville.

The fishing: When bass fishing Guntersville, anglers should think grass cover. Most lakes in Alabama support water-weed growth, but Guntersville is spectacular in its grass growth. Milfoil grows thick, and the bass love it. Anglers should concentrate on the edges of thick weed growth and use either plastic worms or large soft-plastic tube lures. In the early spring, large light-colored spinner baits and even crankbaits worked along drop-offs and weed bed edges can be quite effective. Underwater stump fields can yield some of the largest bass that are caught. Bass fishing in

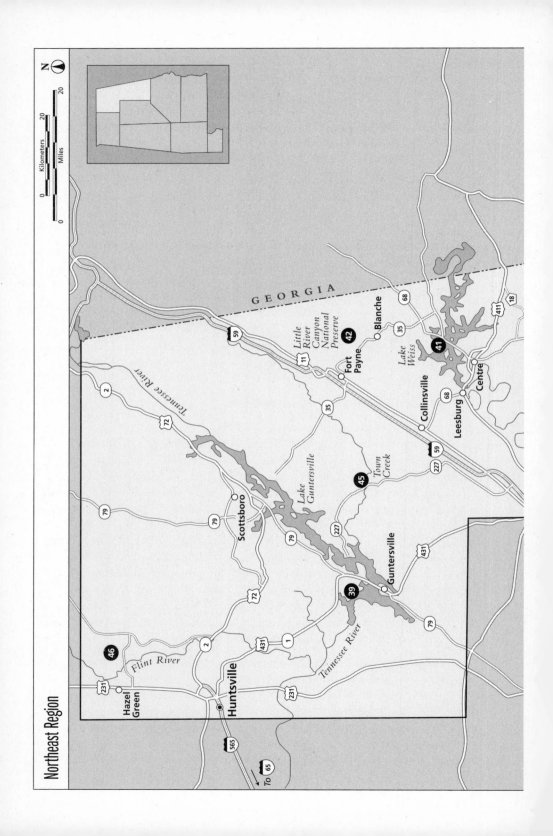

Northeast Region

N

Kilometers
0   20

Miles
0   20

GEORGIA

Little
River
Canyon
National
Preserve

Blanche

Fort Payne

Lake
Weiss

Centre

Collinsville

Leesburg

Tennessee River

Scottsboro

Lake
Guntersville

Town
Creek

Guntersville

Flint River

Hazel
Green

Huntsville

Tennessee River

To 65

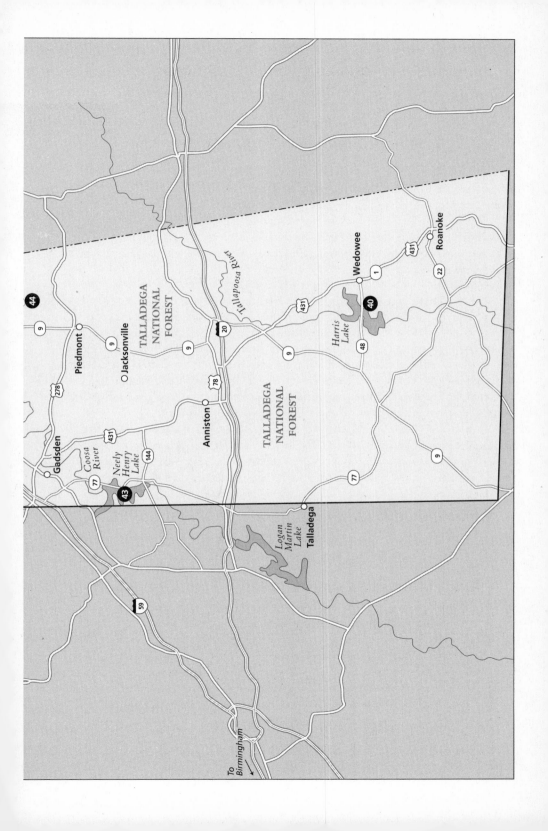

Guntersville is a year-round deal; even in the coldest months, bass fishing is still very good. Guntersville is a good lake to work weedless soft-plastic jerkbaits. These baits will allow anglers to cast into heavy cover and still be able to work the bait and entice a strike. Soft top-water baits such as frogs, mice, and even unweighted worms can be deadly on big bass here. Cast these weedless floaters into small open pockets in the weed mats and hold on. Very often the vicious strike will come just as the bait either enters the little open area or just as it is about to leave the open area. Be ready and set the hook hard! During the winter, anglers have good success on Guntersville by using large spinner baits dropped into deeper water and slowly rolled across bottom structure. Be prepared to hang up and lose a few baits, but also be prepared to have some big bass take your spinner, too. Another good winter tactic is to find creek channels that lead up to shallow flats and work these submerged creeks with either spoons or lipless crankbaits in shad colors. Good concentrations of bass can be found this way as they prepare to go up on the warmer flats for their spring spawn. This can happen as early as March or even the end of February if the winter has been mild and a few warm rains have fallen.

Although bass fishing gets the greatest attention at Guntersville, the other fishing options are very good, also. Crappie fishing is great during the spring. Any of the many feeder creeks will have a heavy run of crappie in late March and April; the weather will determine exact timing. Anglers who have a bucket of minnows and some patience will be able to track the crappie down. Some good creeks to try for spring crappie are Dry Creek, Jones Creek, Coon Creek, and Long Island Cove on the south side of the lake. On the north side, anglers should try Big Spring Creek, Sauty Creek, and Mud Creek. These all have good crappie runs.

Both stripers and hybrid stripers can also be caught up the various feeder creeks in the spring. Anglers will be able to find these fish anywhere from the creek mouths in the main lake all the way up to the first impassible shoal. The fish will move constantly in the creek, but they will respond when a shad look-alike comes in front of them.

Some very big catfish are caught every year in Lake Guntersville. Anglers who are in search of catfish should try prepared commercial catfish baits, but large live shad are also very good, especially for the bigger fish. For Old Whiskers, try to work fairly deep creek and river channels, especially those that show steep bluffs and drop-offs.

Finally, anglers should find a shady shoreline, and bream of many kinds will be there. Crickets and worms are the old reliable bream baits, but catalpa worms when they can be found are very good on bedding bream. Catfish love catalpa worms, too, so be prepared. A truly fun way to fish for Guntersville bream is use a fly rod and a small yellow popping bug.

Even though the outstanding bass fishing is the main reason most anglers make the trip to Guntersville, there are just so many different kinds of fish and ways to fish for them, this huge lake deserves a good long multi-look to explore its possibilities.

DeLorme: *Alabama Atlas & Gazetteer:* Page 19 H10; page 20 D5; page 25 A10, page 26 A1.

Camping and lodging: There are many options. Almost every possible kind of angler housing is available in the Guntersville area. Lake Guntersville State Park is an absolutely first-rate facility with camping ranging from primitive sleep-on-the-ground tent camping to very upscale lodge and chalet facilities. The price is very reasonable, also. Reservations are strongly encouraged because during the season, rooms are booked for months in advance. Also, Guntersville State Park has very good launch facilities. This is a great family-oriented place to stay. Very good campgrounds are at Siebold Creek Recreation Area and Goose Pond on the upper regions.

A very nice option, and one I highly recommend for visiting anglers, is on Spring Creek at the Tennessee Valley Floating Condominiums (866-582-0015). These tidy little house-boat units allow anglers to launch their boats, fish hard all day, and then come back and tie the boat up right at the rail of the condo. In the morning, anglers can eat breakfast, step out on the deck, step into the boat, and off they go! Also, it's really sort of nice to be able to cook supper, watch the ball game on television, and keep an eye on a bobber right off the back porch. It's fun to have a meal interrupted by a nice fat crappie or catfish that decides to visit. For anglers with their own boats, this has got to be about the best housing situation possible!

Tips and cautions: Most serious anglers on Guntersville go for pretty stout casting gear with seventeen- to twenty-pound test line. This may seem too heavy, but there

Lake Guntersville features great spots such as this one.

Now, this is a fine pair to win a tournament with.

are bass here big enough to tax even this heavy tackle. Also, anglers should be careful when navigating the lake. There are lots of underwater obstructions, and some of them are right below the surface.

Directions: In the northeast corner of Alabama, Lake Guntersville is between Interstate 65 and Interstate 59 north of Birmingham. Scottsboro, basically the mid-point, is on U.S. Highway 72 and is a good starting location. On the south end of the lake, the town of Guntersville offers very many access points, and U.S. Highway 431 is the best route to this area.

For more information: Alabama Wildlife and Freshwater Fisheries Division; Tennessee Valley Authority.

40 Harris Lake (Lake Wedowee)

Key species: Spotted bass, largemouth bass, crappie, striped bass.

Overview: Harris Lake is the most recently completed electricity generating lake in the state. It is 24 miles long and covers nearly 11,000 acres. It is the first dammed lake in Alabama on the Tallapoosa River.

Description: Harris Lake appears to be a lake in transition because of its relative young age. Gamefish appear to be still establishing themselves, and the carrying capacity of the lake has not been established. For instance, fish populations are fairly high, but there appears to be an overload of smaller fish, especially spotted bass. Since April of 2006, anglers have been encouraged to keep smaller spotted bass to help better balance the spotted bass population. Crappie appear to be doing very well with some very large crappie being taken in study samples. Largemouth bass seem to be in good shape.

The fishing: Harris Lake is reported to have some very big largemouth bass. If the spotted bass population seems to be heavy on undersize fish, the largemouth bass seem to be doing quite well. The lake itself seems to have good quality, relatively cool water for summer fishing, which makes for good open-water schooling action for bass and stripers. Especially in low-light conditions (early, late, cloudy, rainy), bass are very commonly found in roving schools chasing shad. Other good places to look for big bass are around main body structures such as river channel bends, sharp points, and creek channels. For these places plastic baits, spinner baits, and even heavy chrome-finish spoons are good. Night fishing is good for bass on Harris Lake, but anglers must be careful. Lots of still standing timber and underwater wood make night fishing an adventure.

Lake Harris largemouth bass grow quickly and large.

There is a good winter fishery for largemouth bass in Harris Lake. In fact, some of the largest bass are taken during the colder months. The big fish seem to be very willing to bite, and they don't seem particular about lures. Traditional deeper water baits such as plastic worms fished slowly as well as lipless crankbaits moved quickly around bluffs and drop-offs have all produced big wintertime fish. Anglers should come prepared. Even though this is Alabama in the deep South, winter winds can be cold. It might be a good idea to put slightly heavier line on your reel during the winter. The fish seem to run bigger, and the standing timber and other cover below the water are just a little bit closer since winter water levels tend to be lower.

Crappie tend to grow big in Harris Lake, and they are found near deeper vertical structure. Minnows, jigs, and even small spoons that resemble smaller shad are good on the crappie. Anglers might want to try night fishing for crappie under lights. This is a very relaxing way to load up an ice chest with great-tasting fish.

DeLorme: Alabama Atlas & Gazetteer: Page 33 H8.

Camping: The closest public camping area is Cheaha State Park, perhaps 30 miles northwest of Harris Lake. It is a very nice facility with full hook-up and primitive campgrounds. Sites range from $10 to $16 per night. Call (251) 488-5114 for reservations, which are strongly urged.

Tips and cautions: If fishing at night, Harris Lake regulations require anglers to use running lights at all times.

Directions: From Birmingham take Interstate 20 east. Go past Anniston, then exit south on U.S. Highway 431/Highway 1. When you get to Wedowee, go west on Highway 48. This will lead right to the lake.

For more information: Alabama Wildlife and Freshwater Fisheries Division.

41 Lake Weiss

Key species: Crappie, largemouth bass, striped bass.

Overview: Lake Weiss is a dammed lake created by the blocking of the Coosa River. The lake is a large impoundment covering more than 30,000 acres in northeast Alabama and projecting into Georgia to the east.

Description: Lake Weiss claims the title "Crappie Capital of the World," and judging by the numbers and size of crappie that come from the lake, the title may be very accurate. People come every year from all over the country and even around the world to sample the fast and steady crappie bite here. Study results project that Lake Weiss has a huge number of crappie just under the legal size of 10 inches, so this fishery should continue to be very strong. There are a number of places along roadsides, docks, and other land-based areas where bank anglers can have good success.

There are four free public access areas and at least thirty-seven private marinas on the lake. The immediate area has several campgrounds, motels, restaurants, and other service facilities. Lake Weiss is surrounded by communities that cater to the

This is a very cold early spring morning! The bass were hot, though.

angler. Since Lake Weiss is a major economic power in Cherokee County, the residents and businesses of this area are very friendly toward visiting anglers, and most will go out of their way to help anglers.

The fishing: Crappie are the main focus of Lake Weiss, but by no means are "speckled perch" the only target for anglers. There is a very good largemouth bass fishery on Lake Weiss, and the striped bass fishing can be very good.

For crappie, regardless of the season, live minnows are always good when fished around trees, stumps, docks, and other structure. Many crappie experts on Lake Weiss like to troll small dark-colored jigs around structure and shallower creek channels for good results. Very small Beetle-spins fished slowly around trees and other structure can be good in the early spring when the crappie are just forming up to run to shallower flats and creeks. When one crappie is caught, the angler should mark the location, depth, and bait; where there is one crappie, there will be more. There are plenty of bait and tackle shops around Lake Weiss, so obtaining a good supply of lively minnows should never be a problem. Lee Pitts (256-422-3787 or 256-390-4145), a very well-recommended guide and the operator of Pitt Stop Bait and Tackle on Lake Weiss, tells me that the crappie season usually begins in earnest in late February and early March. He says that crappie will start to move up Big Nose Creek and Little Nose Creek in March and April where they really stack up for spawning. Although spring is the hottest time for crappie, they never completely shut down in Lake Weiss as they do in many lakes. In warmer or colder weather, anglers seeking a heavy stringer of slabs should look for deep cover; 15 to

30 feet is a good depth to start. Slowly fish the depths near old trees and other vertical structure until the depth the crappie are holding at is found.

Lake Weiss bass seem to prefer old creek and river channels, depending on the time of year, with spinner and buzz baits being very effective, especially during the spring season. Lee Pitts says that spring bass fishing at Lake Weiss is about as easy as it ever gets; the bass get very aggressive when they go on the beds. He particularly recommends fishing shallow water bank grass with top-waters and buzz baits. The bass will really come out of the water in the spring! Creek mouths worked with fairly large spinner baits can be very good. Don't overlook causeways and other developed shorelines. Weiss bass like to hang around solid structure, such as bridge supports and roadway boulders. When the bass are holding on solid structure, a lipless crankbait run quickly past the structure, and sometimes even touching the structure, can bring very good results.

For the stripers, look for schools of shad on the depth finder or fish breaking water in the middle of the lake. Early in the day in the main river channel, stripers will chase shad until the sun gets high, and then they tend to drop down into channel side structure such as timber and old roadbeds, where anglers send live shad down to about 10 to 14 feet. Regardless of the season and time of day, the stripers will be where the shad are. Good results on the big line-siders can happen when live shad are dropped into deeper water where the stripers are showing on fish-finder screens. Use just enough weight to take the bait down to the level where stripers are holding.

Lake Weiss is the Crappie Capital of the World!

DeLorme: Alabama Atlas & Gazetteer: Page 27 D7.

Camping: Anglers can find campsites at Riverside Campground at Cedar Bluff; (256) 779-8365. For a more refined stay, try Chestnut Bay Resort; (256) 526-7778.

Tips and cautions: Special rules for Lake Weiss: 1. No crappie less than 10 inches can be kept. 2. Up to thirty white bass, yellow bass, striped bass, or hybrid bass may be kept. 3. No more than one day's creel limit of gamefish can be transported out of state.

Captain Lee warns visiting anglers to be aware that during winter, or any other time that the water level is down, many old house foundations, stair steps, and other hard leftover stuff is exposed or very shallow. This stuff can surely tear up an outboard lower unit, so anglers need to keep an eye on the depth finder and try to stay in the channels or creek beds. Most fish in low-water conditions will be in the deeper channels, anyway. Just be careful about taking shortcuts across points and flats.

Directions: From Birmingham, take Interstate 59 north to Collinsville. Turn right onto Highway 68 from Collinsville to the lake. Leesburg and Centre are good towns to base a fishing trip from.

For more information: Alabama Wildlife and Freshwater Fisheries Division.

Good Eats

Lee Pitts says that Starr's Barbecue and Tony's Steak house, both in Centre, are very good places for hungry anglers to fill up with good food.

42 Little River Canyon

Key species: Redeye bass, spotted bass, bream, occasional rainbow trout.

Overview: A very, very wild, rough, and rugged place is Little River Canyon. The actual canyon starts below the 45-foot-high falls and ends about 12 miles downstream where the river leaves the rugged country behind.

Description: The canyon itself runs up to a half mile wide and 600 feet deep. At the bottom is Little River, which flows through massive boulders, waterfalls, rapids, and calm, deeper pools. This is not a place for the weak of heart or weak of leg. Getting to the river in the canyon will involve a considerable hike, and there are some massive cliffs that must be dealt with. There is absolutely no boat use in Little River Canyon. Expect to see a wide range of wildlife in the canyon; peregrine falcons and bald eagles nest there. There is river above and below the canyon, and fishing can be quite good in both places. However, the wildness and beauty of the Little River Canyon makes it a place like no other.

If you are an angler who wants to escape from the crowd and boldly go where perhaps no angler has gone before, Little River may be the place for you. Although the best fishing is probably at Canyon Mouth Park (day use only) where the river

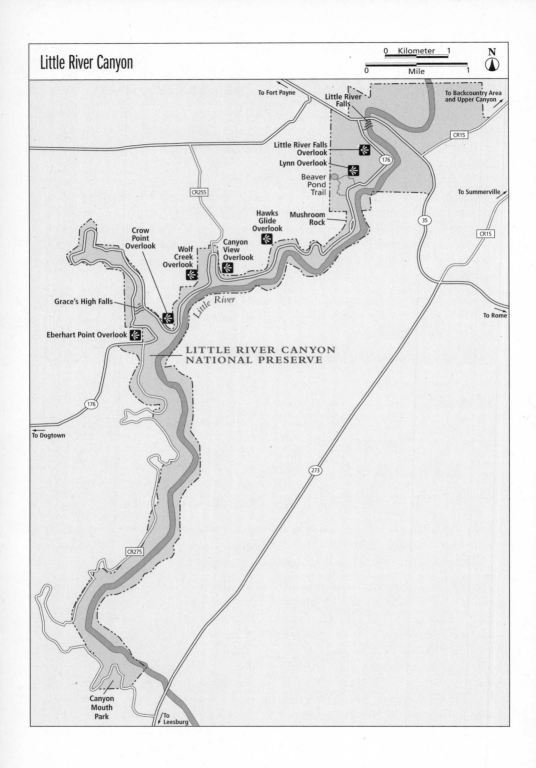

Little River Canyon

0   Kilometer   1
0   Mile   1

N

To Fort Payne

Little River
Falls

To Backcountry Area
and Upper Canyon

CR15

Little River Falls
Overlook

Lynn Overlook

176

Beaver
Pond
Trail

To Summerville

CR255

Hawks
Glide
Overlook

Mushroom
Rock

35

CR15

Crow
Point
Overlook

Canyon
View
Overlook

Wolf
Creek
Overlook

Little River

Grace's High Falls

LITTLE RIVER CANYON
NATIONAL PRESERVE

To Rome

Eberhart Point Overlook

176

To Dogtown

273

CR275

Canyon
Mouth
Park

To
Leesburg

Little River Canyon is a wild and beautiful place to go fishing!

exits the canyon, there is just something about the deep gorge, spectacular cliffs, and roaring water inside the canyon that will draw a certain type of angler. Probably just fishing the place will be more of an attraction than any fish that are caught. Be sure and take a good supply of tackle, bait, and other fishing equipment because there are absolutely no resupply sources at the bottom of the gorge. There are a number of pull-offs and parking areas along Rim Road, which runs parallel to the canyon below Little River Falls, but all access points require a considerable hike in, and, of course, a hike out—uphill. The National Preserve does not allow camping in the lower canyon so the hike in and out must be done in one day, but there are primitive camping spots north of Highway 35 in the backcountry area that allow anglers to stay overnight. These campsites are on a first-come, first-serve basis, with no reservations taken.

Needless to say, any fishing excursion to Little River Canyon will require caution and good judgment. A fall with an injury at the bottom of the gorge could be disastrous; there are no roads in, and there is no river traffic at all. A good access point is the Eberhart Point Overlook, where there is a pull-off and an old roadbed that leads to the water. Good specific maps and directions can be obtained from the Little River Canyon National Preserve Web site (see Appendix).

The fishing: This is wilderness fishing, and the Little River flow can vary widely from a trickle in the dry summer to a wild and extremely dangerous torrent in the winter and spring and after heavy rains. Water flow will dictate fishing. When the water is low, anglers should fish the deeper and slower pools, especially the head-waters, using smaller in-line spinners such as Mepps and Rooster tails. These lures should gather in the stream bass (redeyes and spotted bass) and also the bream that live in the shady bank areas under the overhanging branches. Reliable sources report that some very nice redbreast bream are in Little River.

In certain of the cooler pools, rainbow trout that have escaped from upstream plantings on the East Fork of Little River in Georgia can sometimes be encountered, but this is far from certain. If an angler makes the trip in and should happen to catch a rainbow trout, well, that's just some pretty good fortune and should be a treasured moment.

Basically, Little River is a typical mountain stream with typically smaller bass and bream; it just happens to occupy a spectacular valley gorge. The attraction of fishing this place is that the fish will most likely never have seen a bait before. Craw-fish imitations such as small plastic worms on one-eighth ounce jig heads worked slowly around boulders are very good. For the surest bet, find a still, shallow back-water and roll over rocks to find small crawfish. Put a 2-inch crawfish on a small hook, drop it in the water, and if there is anything around, it will eat the crawfish.

Again, be sure and take everything as far as fishing equipment goes that you might need, but don't take any excess stuff. Remember that everything you carry

Little River Falls at the head of the canyon.

in going downhill in the morning, you'll have to haul out uphill in the evening. It is a balancing act. Take all that you think you'll need and spares, but know that anything not used is just that much extra weight to haul out in the evening. For sure, a good supply of drinking water and some energy bars need to go with any hiking angler in Little River Canyon.

DeLorme: Alabama Atlas & Gazetteer: Page 27 A7.

Camping: There is no camping in the Little River Canyon. Hike in and hike out is the rule. Fort Payne is probably the closest place to stay.

Tips and cautions: Be aware that there are snakes in the canyon, and loose rocks and steep trails will be encountered. Also, make sure someone knows where you are going and when you will return. This is a serious thing; it is not a stroll in the park.

Directions: From Gadsden, take Interstate 59 northeast. At Fort Payne, exit onto Highway 35 toward Blanche. Direction signs for the Little River Canyon National Preserve will be on Highway 35.

For more information: Little River Canyon National Preserve.

43 Neely Henry Lake

Key species: Largemouth bass, spotted bass, crappie, striped bass, hybrid striped bass.

Overview: Covering more than 11,000 acres, Neely Henry offers a fine assortment of fishing options. The lake stretches for more than 77 miles up from Neely Henry Dam and gives anglers a wide range of choice for fishing. From City Park up, Neely Henry is essentially a river, and it needs to be fished as a river.

Description: Since this lake is located between two other fine fishing lakes, Weiss and Logan Martin, sometimes Neely Henry is overlooked by anglers. This is a mistake, because Neely Henry is a fine place to get into some very hot fishing. Another of the fabulous Alabama Coosa River lakes, Neely Henry is quite easy to get to and offers a range of launch options and locations for anglers. Studies indicate that fish populations in Neely Henry Lake are higher than state average, while the overall health of gamefish is very good. Spotted bass in the 14- to 20-inch range are very high in numbers. Crappie in Neely Henry reach a foot in length in only two years. There is good fishing below the dam.

The fishing: A good thing to keep in mind when fishing Neely Henry is that the feeder creeks and streams are often the best places to find fish. Ohatchee Creek and Cane Creek are very good spots for stripers and hybrid stripers during the spring spawning run. When hybrids, whites, and stripers pile up at a creek shoal, any bait that matches the general size and color of shad at that time will gather in the fish. Silver lipped plugs, smaller crankbaits in chrome finish, and, of course, white jigs and spinners will work. Hook the largest crappie minnows that can be found through the lips and drift them with just enough weight to take the minnows down

Below the dam is also a great place to fish.

as the boat drifts downstream with the current; it's a great way to locate just where the stripers and hybrids are holding.

Crappie are not quite as big or thick as in Lake Weiss, but there are still lots of them here. Small (one quarter to one sixteenth ounce) jigs in dark colors can be quite effective on crappie. Look for spawning fish in shallow structure such as blown-down trees or limbs that have fallen off overhanging trees. Willow trees are very good places to start a crappie hunt. Of course, a couple of light action rods with eight-pound line and lively minnows on small hooks lowered close to structure is the best way to start a collection of crappie. When a crappie is caught, try to determine the exact depth and situation so the pattern can be established.

Bass are caught on spinner baits and buzz baits worked close to cover. Sometimes, soft plastics worked on or near the bottom in steep cover such as cliffs and bluffs will be the ticket. Lee Pitts, who guides on Neely Henry when he's not guiding on Lake Weiss, says that bass anglers will need to look for underwater timber (there is lots of it) and work these spots well. He also says that shoals in the sharper bends of the main river channel can be very good. However, the most important thing in Neely Henry is the current, or the lack of it. When the dam is pumping water, a definite current is created in Neely Henry Lake upstream, and this current really turns on the bass. It also helps concentrate the bigger fish near structure on the main river channel, where they ambush bait. When the dam is not pumping, the fish are still there and they still can be caught; it is just slower and anglers have to work harder because the fish are much more spread out. When the water starts moving, it's as if a switch were turned on and the bass start actively feeding.

During the summer, watch for open-water action when stripers chase shad on top. A Spook or silver Devil's Horse cast near break stripers can produce some big fish and good fun.

DeLorme: Alabama Atlas & Gazetteer: Page 26 H3.

Here's a typical Neely Henry hybrid bass.

Feeder creeks are great spring spots for hybrids and stripers.

Camping and lodging: A wide range of motel accommodations are available in Gadsden.

Tips and cautions: There is a limit of three rods to be used by any single angler at one time when fishing on Neely Henry Lake.

Directions: From Birmingham, take Interstate 59 north to Gadsden. From Gadsden take Highway 77 south, then go right on Highway 144, cross the dam, and you'll see the ramps on the right.

For more information: Alabama Wildlife and Freshwater Fisheries Division.

44 Terrapin Creek

Key species: Largemouth bass, spotted bass, redeye bass, several kinds of sunfish; striped bass are occasionally caught in the lower reaches, especially in the spring.

Overview: This creek starts in the Talladega National Forest in Cleburne County and flows through both Calhoun and Cherokee Counties before it joins the Coosa River. It presents a changing picture to anglers as it moves and gradually picks up size and water flow.

Description: This little jewel of a creek has something for everyone who fishes. As it joins the Coosa, it is typical Alabama river fishing, and tackle needs to be somewhat heavier. At the upper end, two smaller streams, South Fork and Little Terrapin, join to form Terrapin Creek, and fishing gear needs to reflect the smaller water, smaller fish situation there.

Terrapin Creek is a small foothill stream that becomes a small river. No matter where it is fished, good fishing is present along its entire length. Some sections of the creek just take a little more work to get to. A small flat-bottom boat, canoe, or kayak will be very helpful in the lower reaches of the creek. As with any creek, anglers should watch for heavy flow after rains. When the water is up, Terrapin Creek can really roll along, so exercise caution, especially in shoal areas.

Either wading or floating, a day spent on Terrapin Creek will probably be a day to remember, both for fish caught and for scenery enjoyed.

The fishing: In the upper reaches, ultra-light tackle (six-pound line) and small baits are the best way to go. Wading is the best way to get on the creek. Be sure and have good footwear, and watch for slick or loose rocks. You don't want to break something important like a rod or a leg up there in the hills.

The fish in the upstream sections will typically be found near the shore: in shady places under overhanging limbs, and in pockets of water behind rocks and

North Alabama creeks are wonderful in the spring.

boulders. The creek bass here will also respond well to small dark-colored in-line spinners and small beetle-spins. Anglers can expect to gather a mixed bag of fish. The spotted bass and redeye bass will be mingled in with red-belly bream and goggle eyes. Some respectable largemouth bass are caught in unlikely small places on Terrapin Creek; be ready.

As the creek grows larger, from say County Road 8 to the Highway 9 Bridge near Ellisville, several float trips of various length and duration are possible. Here the water gets a bit bigger, and so do the fish. Light spinning gear, eight- to ten-pound line, will work here. Crawfish imitations and dark-colored soft-plastic tube lures and jigs work well. Live bait, such as minnows and especially crawfish, are always good. A small crawfish hooked through the tail and tossed into deeper pockets and holes behind structure will quickly indicate if fish are there and hungry.

DeLorme: Alabama Atlas & Gazetteer: Page 27 F7.

Camping: No camping areas close. Arrangements might be made with private landowners. The best bet for camping would be at Weiss Lake. Several motels can be found at Centre.

Tips and cautions: Maps of Talladega National Forest can be very helpful in locating creek crossings of roads, and they can be obtained from the USDA Forest Service or

Aggressive creek bass take spinners eagerly.

area outdoor stores. Exercise caution after heavy rains. Even rain far upstream can create dangerous water conditions downstream.

Directions: From Piedmont, take Highway 9 north toward Centre. Less than 5 miles up Highway 9 is a good put-in spot for a float trip. Canoe or kayak shuttle services are available in the area.

For more information: Talladega National Forest; Alabama Wildlife and Freshwater Fisheries Division.

45 Town Creek

Key species: Spotted bass, redeye bass, largemouth bass, various bream, catfish.

Overview: Town Creek starts in eastern Dekalb County and runs almost the entire width of the county before it flows into Lake Guntersville. It is a clear, rather fast moving stream that is a delight to see.

Description: Town Creek requires anglers to exercise some caution. The shoreline is basically rock, and when wet, these rocks can be very slick. There are also some sharp drop-offs, so wading must be done with care. Just below the Highway 227 crossing, there is a remarkably attractive waterfall with a drop of about 10 to 12 feet. This is a gorgeous hole of water! Below this waterfall, the stream continues on with deep holes alternating with rapid runs until the stream runs into Lake Guntersville. Also, anglers should be advised that snakes are abundant on Town Creek. Watch where you put hands and feet! Good solid footwear is a definite requirement when fishing Town Creek. As Town Creek nears Lake Guntersville, it broadens and becomes more of a backwater bay. This is not all bad; some very good spotted bass call these final miles of Town Creek home. Where the creek enters Guntersville, a boat of some sort would be most helpful.

For those anglers who love to fish creeks, this stream deserves attention. Access to Town Creek is pretty limited, and no float trip shuttle options are available. It is basically a walk-in/walk-out fishery. There are some outstanding waterfalls and shoals on the creek. Of course, in deep summer dry times, the water level in Town Creek will fall considerably, so anglers should make sure enough water is flowing to make a trip worthwhile.

The fishing: The clear, fast water promises something nice, and it doesn't disappoint. A good population of redeye bass, spotted bass, and largemouth bass in the lower reaches are present. It may take awhile for an angler to find out what sort of bait the fish want. Small in-line spinners like Rooster tails and Mepps are usually effective. Small, one-quarter to one-eighth ounce jigs in brown and chartreuse with small plastic worm trailers can be quite effective. Basically, anything that looks like a crawfish is a good bet. In the slower, deeper sections, live bait, like crawfish and minnows, drifted along the bottom can yield very nice fish. Don't be surprised if a channel catfish shows up; they live here, too.

Nice redeye bass hold at the foot of the falls.

There are lots of red-belly and long-ear sunfish in Town Creek, and they are almost always cooperative. Look for these beautiful creek bream in the shadows of overhanging tree limbs where they wait for some unlucky insect to fall into the water. Toss a small top-water bait or fly into the shadows, and the bream may fight one another to get at your bait. During the spring, these creek bream will find sunny, open shallows off the main creek current to bed up. A worm on a small gold hook drifted with just a tiny split-shot for weight can be deadly on the bream.

Any more than six-pound line is too big for this stream. Most bass will be less than three pounds, but a three-pound bass in this fast current is a pleasure. A very neat thing about the bass in Town Creek is that when an angler hooks one, almost always another bass will follow the hooked fish up.

If an angler is lucky enough to get on Town Creek early or late in the day, small top-water lures such as Rapalas, Tiny Torpedos, and others can be very effective in the shady areas near overhanging limbs. A fly rod with a small grasshopper popping bug might be the ultimate kind of fun on this small creek.

DeLorme: Alabama Atlas & Gazetteer: Page 26 A3.

Camping: None close. Probably the best option is Lake Guntersville State Park about 30 miles away.

Tips and cautions: Please be careful when wading this creek. The rocks can shift and they are always slick when wet. Of course, don't leave trash or fishing line behind.

Pack it all out, and even bring out trash someone else has left.

Directions: From Lake Guntersville State Park, take Highway 227 east until Town Creek is crossed. The bridge is new and high; it's obvious when you are there. A good pull-off is just past the bridge, and an old road leads down to the water. An old destroyed mill foundation and ruin is right at the high waterfall and is a good landmark.

For more information: Alabama Wildlife and Freshwater Fisheries Division.

46 Flint River

Key species: Smallmouth bass, spotted bass, largemouth bass, bream of several kinds.

Overview: The Flint is a lovely river to float and fish. It doesn't run as far as some rivers: only about 50 miles from its headwaters up in Tennessee to its merging with the Tennessee River in Madison County. Along the way anglers will be able to cast to a wide range of structure and water conditions, all of which may hold fish.

Description: The Flint River water clarity can vary greatly in a short period of time. After heavy rains, the water will muddy and become almost unfishable. It usually clears after a few days' run-off. The streamside vegetation can be spectacular in spring with wildflowers thick and brilliant. Naturally, float anglers must be aware of current and obstructions. There are no severe rapids or drop-offs on the Flint, but there are shoals that could present problems if a boat were to get sideways on them. Keep the boat headed toward the "V" of the fast water, and all should be well.

A very large number of fish species are present; many are unnoticed except by fishery biologists doing surveys, but there are plenty of gamefish to keep anglers busy on a float. There are some fishable side-streams that flow into the Flint. Anglers should budget a little time to investigate these feeder creeks. There are log-jams that anglers must deal with. It goes without saying, the Flint is not the place to try to put in an expensive bass boat and motor. This is float fishing, and a johnboat, canoe, or kayak would be the boat of choice.

The fishing: Any river that is home to smallmouth bass is a good river to me. The Flint does have brownies, and they can be very agreeable to fighting with an angler. Most of the bass are in the pound to three-pound range, but there are larger fish here. Six- to ten-pound line is fine. Crawfish imitations are good, and a small jig (one-eighth to one-quarter ounce) with a 3-inch crawfish-colored plastic worm on the hook fished around underwater boulders and other structure in moving water is a good way to find a smallmouth. Small crawfish imitation crankbaits are good, too. Try to run these tiny crankbaits as close to underwater structure as possible. If the bait bangs the rock or log, great. The strike often comes right after the lure hits something. Early and late or on dark and cloudy days, small Rebel and Rapala crankbaits (I like gold finishes) tossed up under vegetation that overhangs the water and casts a shadow can be very productive. Smallmouth bass on top-waters is fishing at its best.

Largemouth and spotted bass are here, too. They tend to be in slower waters off the main river, especially the largemouths. Be sure and investigate some of the feeder creeks. Spotted bass may be shoulder to shoulder with the brownies in the main river current. They all like crawfish, and soft-plastic tube baits tossed up into pockets and backwaters can bring any of the bass species out.

The bream are thick in Flint River. They respond to live bait, of course, but they like small in-line spinners such as Roostertails in bright colors, too. Sometimes, a black Roostertail is the ticket for panfish. You may need to experiment to find the size and color they want. Don't be surprised if your bream fishing experiment is interrupted by a bass who finds your "bream" bait too attractive to pass up.

For those anglers who are skilled in the art, probably the most fun form of fishing the Flint will be fly fishing. A dark Woolybugger allowed to sink into shadow and near rocks can attract a lot of attention. Probably the most fun of all is casting popping bugs near to shoreline cover and under overhanging limbs. Even skilled casters lose baits here, but the sight of a fat bream or an angry bass smashing a popper makes up for the loss!

DeLorme: Alabama Atlas & Gazetteer: Page 19 A8, B9.

Camping: There is no public camping near the river, but Flint River Canoe Rentals (256-858-2280) allows camping to folks who either rent boats from them or use their shuttle service (highly recommended for floaters and anglers).

Tips and cautions: As on any float stream, anglers on the Flint should pay attention to the weather, and if heavy rain is predicted, fish somewhere else.

Directions: From Huntsville, take U.S. Highway 231 to the town of Hazel Green. Turn right (east) on Joe Quick Road. This will cross the Flint and give access.

For more information: Alabama Wildlife and Freshwater Fisheries Division.

Northwest Region

This is a wonderful part of the state because of its big, clear lakes and its small, clear streams. Anglers will find some of the best fishing in the world for a number of species in the northwest section of Alabama. Along with the fishing, there are some fine cities and towns full of interesting things for non-anglers to enjoy.

When fishing the big lakes—Wheeler, Wilson, and Pickwick—in this region, anglers should be aware that these lakes are very much influenced by the flow of water between one lake and the next, and that water levels and flow can change quickly. Particularly, anglers fishing immediately below the dams must be very careful. These massive dams release a lot of water quickly, and the conditions can get rough. Smallmouth bass fishing in particular is just about as good as it gets anywhere in the world in these big Tennessee River lakes.

The smaller lakes and streams of the northwest region give anglers who wish to escape the noise and bustle of the big lakes wonderful places to observe nature and still have a chance to catch some good fish. Float fishing and small lakes may not produce the world-record catches of the lakes, but they bring their own rewards in the form of quiet, calm fishing and catching. Bear Creek and the Bear Creek Lakes are small places, but they still hold some very good bass and other gamefish.

In short, the northwest region of Alabama offers a whole lot of fishing in many different formats. No matter if you prefer to fly around big lakes on super-powered bass boats or drift down a peaceful stream in a canoe, this area provides some really great fishing.

Finally, some of the finest state parks can be found in this region. Joe Wheeler State Park, in particular, is a joy. Great housing, lots of facilities, wonderful and plentiful boat ramps, and lots of wildlife to observe and all at very reasonable cost make this park a great place to visit.

It's easy to get to great fishing up here, so pack the car, load the boat, and head on up north to the northwest region of Alabama.

47 Bear Creek Lakes

Key species: Largemouth bass, smallmouth bass, spotted bass, striped bass, channel catfish, bream.

Overview: Simply put, these lakes and the streams connecting them are jewels. There are four fishable lakes and five campgrounds in the Management Area, and they offer anglers a chance to get away from the noise and bustle of the larger, more popular lakes in the state while still having a very good chance at catching a large fish.

Description: There are four lakes: Bear Creek Reservoir, less than 700 acres; Little Bear Lake, 1,560 acres with good stump fields; Upper Bear Lake, 1,850 acres with good standing timber; and Cedar Creek Lake, 4,200 acres. Each lake seems to have

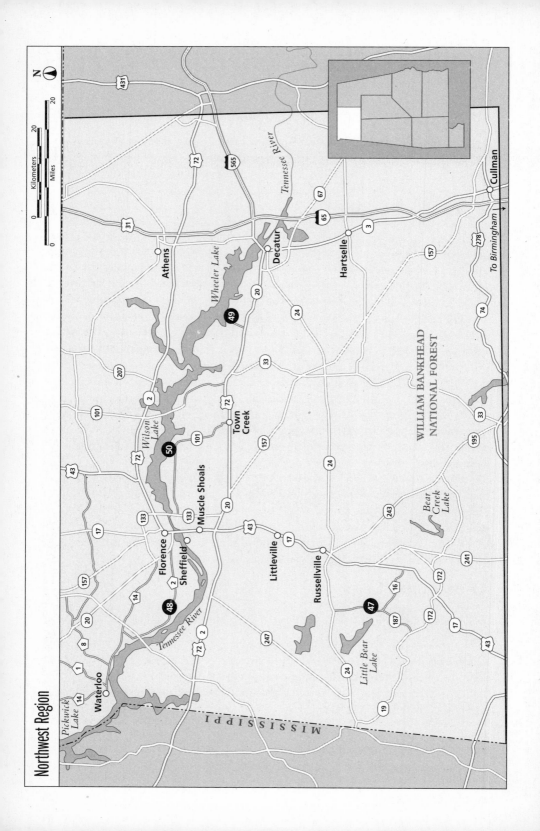

Northwest Region

its own "personality," and anglers should budget enough time to give each lake a try to see what each offers. There are some very large bass in the Bear Creek lakes; the record largemouth bass to date is fifteen pounds ten ounces, and several ten- to twelve-pound fish are caught annually. Very light fishing pressure makes the quality of fishing here high. These lakes deserve the attention of serious anglers, especially those who enjoy getting away from the big crowds on some of the more famous area lakes.

Facilities are very good, launch ramps are on each lake, and the campgrounds are well-maintained and offer many services to campers. Very clear, clean water and no pollution make the lakes very popular for swimming at the camping areas. These are prime family-friendly, multiple-use fishing areas.

The fishing: In Little Bear Lake, smallmouth bass do well, and should be sought near rocks, boulders, and vertical bluffs. Baits that resemble crawfish work well. Smallmouth bass respond well to vertically worked jigs near structure. In Upper Bear Lake, spotted bass, largemouth bass, and smallmouth bass have been stocked and all do well. Anglers should work the standing timber with crankbaits, spinner baits, and plastics on the bottom. Spinner baits catch all three bass species. In the largest lake, Cedar Creek Lake, anglers should again target the standing timber with standard bass baits. A good technique to employ is to cast spinner baits past

Bear Creek Lakes bass are thick, and there are some big ones, too.

In-line spinners take many bass.

structure and then retrieve the bait so that it just contacts the structure, breaking the steady rhythm of the retrieve. Bass often explode on the spinner when it bounces off the limb or rocks.

Stripers often are seen chasing shad in the open waters of the main lake bodies. At these times, top-water lures that are finished in white or chrome colors work well.

Bream should be targeted in the backwaters and shallower banks. Very small jigs and in-line spinners work on bream. Due to the clear and relatively cool water, the Bear Creek Lakes resemble waters of much more northerly states, even Canada, to some anglers. Each lake has very good launch ramp facilities.

DeLorme: Alabama Atlas & Gazetteer: Page 22 A4.

Camping: Excellent. There are 160 campsites, which offer campers a full range of options. Campsite fees vary from $7.50 to $15.00 per night depending on services needed. Most campsites have full electrical and water hookups and laundry facilities. Campground stores are provided.

Tips and cautions: Small craft boaters can use Bear Creek itself on the weekends when the authorities release water from the dam to increase water flow. Canoeists and kayakers should exercise extreme caution. Two sets of rapids on Bear Creek, Upper Factory Falls and Lower Factory Falls, are Class V+ rapids and should not be attempted. Most anglers put in below Factory Falls for fishing float trips.

Directions: From the Florence/Muscle Shoals area, take U.S. Highway 43 south through Littleville. It will lead directly to Russellville, where the facilities are located. More information is available at (877) 367-2232.

For more information: Bear Creek Development Authority; Alabama Wildlife and Freshwater Fisheries Division.

48 Pickwick Lake

Key species: Smallmouth bass, largemouth bass, crappie, sauger, striped bass, hybrid bass.

Overview: Pickwick Dam is in Tennessee, but most of the lake area is in Alabama. Pickwick Lake forms the border between Alabama and Mississippi in the extreme northwestern corner of Alabama. A large lake, Pickwick covers nearly 50,000 acres when at full pool.

Description: Pickwick starts out clear and cold as its waters exit high Wilson Dam. The initial stretch of the lake is somewhat like a river—very much so—and the strongly moving current is a prime location for a major smallmouth bass fishery. Some very big smallmouth bass come out of the headwaters of Pickwick Lake. As the lake moves in the old Tennessee River channel, the waters slow and start to warm, and so Pickwick becomes a major largemouth bass fishery.

Although the headwaters of Pickwick are at Wilson Dam in Florence, and therefore are in a highly populated area, the rest of the lake tends to have basically undeveloped shorelines, and, in fact, much of the northern shores of the lake are in the Lauderdale Wildlife Management Area.

Once the metropolitan Florence area is left behind, the lake becomes a much wilder place. Because of wintertime water drawdowns, Pickwick Lake requires a considerable amount of attention from anglers in boats during these low water periods. There are many rocks, secondary channel structures, and other hard items under the water that can tear up an outboard motor.

The fishing: Big smallmouth bass are probably the major draw for anglers at Pickwick. The stretch of river from Wilson Dam just down past Seven Mile Island is

Pickwick bass will take top-water plugs.

some of the best brownie bass fishing in the world. During full pool times, anglers can motor with care up to the dam itself to fish. During winter, this is not advised. The water gets shallow, and the bottom is rock. The big brownies love to eat the shad that are washed down through Wilson Dam, and they get very big from this massive food supply and from fighting the strong currents of the water. Anglers should target big smallmouths by using white or silver-colored soft body jigs drifted downstream with the current. Try to just tick the top of the underwater rocks and other structure with the lure. Hang-ups will happen, but some of these hang-ups will swim off and jump and otherwise kick up a lot of water as they try to get free from the line. Big, light-colored spinner baits will work, especially when they are fished very slowly, with the blade just barely turning over. Try to drop these spinners to the tops of underwater humps and old structures.

Finally, big smallmouths will respond to white or silver top-water lures. Try to find something about the same size as the shad that are coming through the turbines; a Zara Spook is a good thing to start with. Work the top-water across the surface, and hold on. When a big brownie hits a top-water, it can be almost scary!

As the water flows past Seven Mile Island, it begins to slow and warm. From this point on, anglers will meet with a mix of bass species. A smallmouth may come in on one cast, and the next cast may yield a largemouth. This mix of species holds for quite a distance downstream before the largemouth begin to take over and be dominant.

During the spring, bass anglers will find spawning bass in expected places. Largemouths will be in the warmer, shallower backwaters of flats and sloughs while smallmouth will be slightly deeper, say 4 to 6 feet, and on pebbled or rocky bottoms. Smallmouth tend to spawn a bit earlier than largemouths.

Crappie anglers can find heavy concentrations of specks in the spring as they seek out shallow banks in warmer water to spawn. Anglers should look for shorelines with timber cover, brush piles, or fallen timber. If deeper water is close at hand, a promising spot has been found. Most good crappie anglers use live minnows: under a bobber if the water is shallow, on a tight line if the fish are holding deep. Small jigs and spinners will work, too.

An interesting and delicious fishery has developed in Pickwick Lake involving sauger, those slightly smaller cousins of walleye. A good population of sauger has developed in Pickwick, and these sharp-toothed, glassy-eyed fish love to run up to the dam in early spring to spawn and to eat shad. Anglers can target these fish with small shad, smaller jigs (one-quarter to one-half ounce) in light colors, and in-line spinners in white and silver finishes. Sauger will flash up off the bottom to nab a passing bait, but will hold close to the bottom almost all the time. Fish them deep. Sauger is one of my favorite eating fish. The fillets off a typical two-pound sauger won't be too big, but they will be absolutely delicious fried up right!

A very active Pickwick bass leaves the water.

DeLorme: Alabama Atlas & Gazetteer: Page 16 A2, B3, B4, C4, D5, D6.

Camping: McFarland Park below Florence has very good launch facilities and campgrounds. This is a recommended place to start a Pickwick fishing trip. More information can be obtained by contacting the Landerdale County Tourism Bureau.

Tips and cautions: Anglers fishing Pickwick in the Alabama/Mississippi border area must have each specific state's license—no reciprocity! If an angler is caught fishing the Mississippi shoreline with only an Alabama license, it may very quickly become an expensive fishing trip!

Directions: To reach the headwaters of Pickwick, take Highway 157 south from Florence. It will lead directly to the dam site. To reach the lower Pickwick waters, take Highway 20 out of Florence up into Tennessee. Take County Road 1 south out of Savannah, Tennessee, which will lead to Waterloo, Alabama, which has good facilities for anglers.

For more information: Alabama Wildlife and Freshwater Fisheries Division; Tennessee Valley Authority.

49 Wheeler Lake

Key species: Largemouth bass, smallmouth bass, spotted bass, striped bass, hybrid striped bass, crappie, catfish, various bream.

Overview: Big, big, big: Wheeler Lake stretches for more than 60 miles from its headwaters at Guntersville Dam to Wheeler Dam near Rogersville. It presents anglers with a varied landscape of possibilities from riverlike conditions in the headwaters to wide-open lake conditions down toward Wheeler Dam. Along the way, the lake gives anglers many chances at a very wide range of gamefish.

Description: Wheeler is a very popular lake, and there are many marinas, boat ramps, and housing facilities either on or very near the lake. There are a large number of bass tournaments held on Wheeler annually, and the entire area surrounding the Tennessee River lake chain seems to be geared to serve the fishing and boating public. The lake itself is not crystal clear, but it is rarely muddy, either. Anglers will find the water to be just that color that seems to say "Fish are here!" In short, Wheeler is a good, reliable place to go fishing.

The lake resembles its bigger brother, Lake Guntersville, in basic layout and water conditions, although Wheeler does not typically have quite the rampant growth of milfoil and other water plants. There are a number of major feeder streams that provide good fishing options in their own right.

At Decatur City Park off U.S. Highway 72, probably the biggest, best public boat ramps this writer has ever seen are available for anglers. They are absolutely first-rate and have lots of very close parking. It's easy to see that Decatur knows how to make anglers happy. Anglers do need to exercise caution when fishing

Tremendous ramps can be found at Decatur on Lake Wheeler.

around the dams. Below Wheeler Dam in particular, the water can get very rough. The fishing is very good there, but the water released through the dam's power-generating turbines is very wild and rough, and very strong and treacherous currents are created. Below the dams is not good for inexperienced boaters.

The fishing: Wow! Bass fishing on Wheeler can be fantastic at times. Although all three of the major bass species can be found in Wheeler Lake, probably the most commonly caught bass is old Mr. Largemouth. Especially around the world-famous Decatur Flats, largemouth bass congregate in huge numbers, and some of the bass get quite large. In a recent bass tournament, an angler caught seven largemouth, which weighed a total of forty-two pounds. Do the math . . . A six-pound average will win a whole lot of bass tournaments. Spotted bass and especially smallmouth bass tend to be farther down the lake toward the deeper, cooler water near the dam. The shoreline there is more to their liking: deep, steep, and rocky with abundant crawfish for food. Of course, all of the bass species in Wheeler love to eat shad, and there is a fantastically high population of shad in Wheeler. Bass don't have to go far to find food here. Anglers should use fairly large shad look-alike crankbaits, and big light-colored spinner baits work well, too. Work these lures near drop-offs and especially around mid-lake rises, hilltops underwater, and standing timber when it can be found. In the early spring when bass are on beds up in coves, very slowly worked top-water baits such as flukes and other soft-plastic jerk baits can be very effective on bigger bass. As the season progresses, anglers should look for steep shorelines with deep water nearby. Bass use these areas to ambush the massive schools of shad as they move from shallow water to deep, open water.

Stripers and hybrids make some fantastic spring runs up to the Guntersville Dam and below Wheeler Dam. There are some massive stripers in Wheeler, and anglers should be equipped to handle big, strong fish when striper fishing here. Try live shad drifted with the current using only enough weight to get the shad to sink. Be ready! When one of these fish hits, it will be a shock at their strength and power. It will not be a quick catch, either. They will use the strong current to help in their battle against you. Silver spoons, large white bucktail jigs, and chartreuse soft body jigs in one-half to one ounce weights will work on the stripers and hybrids in the spring runs.

Catfish grow to massive size in Wheeler. How about a 111-pound blue catfish: It was the world record at the time, caught in the mid-'90s. There are some very big catfish in Wheeler, and they respond well to big shad, either alive or dead worked in the main lake body around deep points and deep drop-offs. They will often show as large returns on the fish-finder screen right on the bottom. Again, these fish demand serious gear. Eighty- to one-hundred-pound test line and heavy ocean-type reels and rods are the rule for big cats. A buddy told me recently that he hooked a big catfish this spring on standard bass gear, and he fought the fish for thirty minutes before he ever saw it, and the fish broke him off soon after. The fish was over 4 feet long and was much too powerful for his bass equipment. If you are serious about catching catfish on Wheeler, you'd better have some serious equipment.

Lake Wheeler in the morning is a fine place to be.

FISHING ALABAMA

Crappie do very well on Wheeler, and they grow quite fast and large. The shad that feed the bass later feed the crappie in smaller sizes. Some years are just better for crappie than others. For whatever reason, some years the crappie hatch is poor, and that year's fish just don't do well. However, there are always enough crappie from previous and later years that do have good hatches and survival to make up any slack. Live minnows under a bobber and small beetle-spins are good on crappie.

Finally, bream fishing is excellent in the coves and backwaters of Wheeler Lake. My wife and I had a ball catching some big red-belly bream in a little, clear feeder creek that empties into Wheeler near the state park. We used ultra-light spinning gear and small in-line spinners and tiny floating Rapalas. We'd cast out, let the floater sit, and big, fat red-bellies would flash up and smash our lures. It was great fun! The bream fishing in Wheeler can be excellent at all times, but especially in the spring and summer when the fish are in massive spawning beds. In particular, Mallard Creek Public Recreation area toward the Decatur area has some very good bream fishing.

DeLorme: Alabama Atlas & Gazetteer: Page 17 C10; page 19 D1, D2, E3, F4, F5, G6, G7, G8, G9.

Camping and lodging: A very strong point of Wheeler Lake is the wide range of housing facilities. There are nice cabins for rent at the state park at the dam site. Camping is also offered at the dam site facility. At the Wheeler State Park Lodge, located a bit farther up the lake, anglers can stay in very nice, fully equipped, cool, comfortable rooms, and sit on the balcony outside their rooms and watch the lake, swimming pool, and boat docks where they can safely secure their boats for the night. Excellent boat ramps are at the park. All of this can be had for about $70 per night. I recommend this facility very highly; it's nice.

Tips and cautions: Many good guides are ready to help get visiting anglers on fish. I can particularly recommend Rick Sizemore; he works hard to get anglers where the fish are, and he's a nice guy. Contact him at (256) 762-6661.

Directions: From Birmingham, go north on Interstate 65. Exit at Decatur and either go east on Highway 67 and then north to the upper stretches of the lake, or go west on Highway 67 until it intersects with US 72/Highway 20. US 72/Highway 20 runs along the south side of Wheeler Lake and offers many good access points. (Do not confuse this route with US 72/Highway 2, which runs along the north side of the lake.)

For more information: Alabama Wildlife and Freshwater Fisheries Division; Tennessee Valley Authority.

Good Eats

The world around Wheeler Lake is covered with barbecue places. However, one that this writer would like to recommend to anglers is The Hickory Stick in Decatur, right off Highway 72. It's not fancy, but the ribs are great, the sauce is sweet, spicy, and not too hot, and the hush-puppies are very good. It's easy to get to after a day on the water, too.

50 Wilson Lake

Key species: Smallmouth bass, largemouth bass, spotted bass, striped bass, hybrid striped bass, catfish, various bream.

Overview: First impounded in 1925 by the Works Progress Administration (WPA), Wilson Lake is a deep, clear-water lake, and it occupies the space between Wheeler Lake and Pickwick Lake, both much bigger in size. Wilson is only about 17 miles from dam to dam; it's an easy run in a bass boat from end to end.

Description: Wilson Lake offers anglers some of the most attractive-looking shorelines for fishing. Although there are many private homes on the lake, it never looks overdeveloped, and the boat docks and other man-made structures on the lake just provide more fish habitat. Wilson Lake has a fantastic population of shad and crawfish, and anglers should use this to plan artificial lures for gamefish. Sources tell me that the shad population has boomed in the past thirty years, and this food source has also caused the bass and other gamefish population to boom. For visiting anglers, the Florence area that surrounds the Wilson Dam offers supplies, food, housing, and entertainment.

Smaller does not mean less when it comes to fishing Wilson Lake. From its extremely rough headwaters that exit massive Wheeler Dam to the calmer, deeper waters at old Wilson Dam, Wilson Lake offers a wide range of angling possibilities, and the fishing just never seems to stop whatever the season might be. Except for extremely cold days, fishing goes on year-round here. The fish still bite in cold weather; most people just don't want to brave the conditions. For those who do, some excellent winter catches can be made. There are excellent boat launch facilities on Wilson, and the lake is usually never overcrowded with recreational boaters. In particular, Fleet Harbor Ramps at the Wilson Dam site is a very good place to launch; parking is close at hand and plentiful.

The fishing: Bass are the primary target for anglers at Wilson Lake. Some of the biggest smallmouth bass to be found anywhere in the world live in the fast water just below Wheeler Dam, and anglers come from all over the world to fish for trophy smallmouth. By the way, a "trophy" smallmouth in this lake will be something better than five pounds. The brownies get quite a bit bigger than that, so anglers need to be prepared. Most anglers who specifically target big smallmouth in the Wheeler Dam tailrace waters use fifteen- to twenty-pound line on good-quality level-wind reels with good drags. Big brownies in that fast water will overpower poor-quality reels. Also, lots of really big fish, such as stripers and hybrid bass along with big freshwater drum and buffalo fish, come up to the dam, and if one of these is hooked, the battle will be long and hard. Good equipment is required. The big smallmouth in Wilson Lake make a really strong run up to the dam every fall, and this is a very nice time of year to go fishing. The weather is nice, the temperature starts to drop, leaves start to color up, and the big brownies usually tear it up while chasing shad. Live shad or silver spoons and white jigs will work on these fast-water smallmouth.

Be careful when fishing the headwaters of Lake Wilson! There is a strong current!

Largemouth and spotted bass tend to occupy those parts of Wilson Lake downstream from the tailrace waters. Wilson has some of the most inviting deep coves and pockets for bass fishing I've ever seen. My buddy Rick Sizemore and I fished Wilson recently, and we worked deep, steep drop-offs and logs under shore-line tree limbs, which provide shade and cover. Rick emphasizes the importance of shade on Wilson Lake. The water is clear, and if a shoreline has no shade, the fish just won't be there. We cast white flukes, crawfish imitations, and other soft-plastic baits up under the cover and into shadow, and the largemouth were happy to come and play with us. By the way, Rick is probably the best caster I've seen, and a trip with him is very instructional and helpful in improving one's casting technique. Most of our better fish came from under boat docks, which cast a deep shadow for the fish to hide in. We didn't catch any smallmouth on this trip, but we did see a nice one smash into a cloud of shad that was hanging around a fallen treetop. Rick tells me that when the smallmouth are active, some very impressive catches can be made. He says that it's not unusual to catch five or more smallmouths, all going five pounds or bigger, in a day's fishing. Now, that is my kind of smallmouth fishing!

There is a very good spring run of stripers and hybrids from the main lake up to the Wheeler Lake Dam, and anglers use live shad and big shad look-alike baits; soft jigs in one-ounce sizes are good. Pretty heavy line, twenty-pound or more, is needed for these fish, and the hooks must be very strong. Stripers are powerful fish, and in the strong current below the dams, they require stout equipment.

Catfish get big in Wilson, and anglers who go specifically after old Whiskers should work open-water hilltops and ridges that rise to about 15 feet below the surface. The big cats like to lie down-current on the drop-off into deeper water. Big live shad are the ticket for the really big cats.

DeLorme: Alabama Atlas & Gazetteer: Page 17 C7, C8, C9.

Camping and lodging: Camping would probably best be arranged at Wheeler State Park, which offers excellent camping and hotel accommodations. For those who want to go first class, the Shoals Marriot, which is just beside the dam site at Wilson Lake, offers anglers a very upscale place to stay; it might be a good place to bring your spouse for a fishing trip.

Tips and cautions: A good guide would be a plus, at least for the first trip to Wilson Lake. There are several good ones in the area, but my buddy Rick Sizemore is one of the best. Call (256) 762-6661 for information and reservations.

Directions: Pretty easy. From Decatur, take U.S. Highway 72 / Highway 20 west. To reach the Wheeler Dam site, take Highway 101 north at Town Creek. To reach the Wilson Dam site, take US 72 / Highway 20 to intersection with Highway 157. Go north on Highway 133, which will lead directly to the dam.

For more information: Alabama Wildlife and Freshwater Fisheries Division; Tennessee Valley Authority.

Appendix: Additional Information

Government Agencies and Land Managers

Alabama Marine Resources Division
P.O. Box 189
Dauphin Island, AL 36528
(251) 861-2882
www.outdooralabama.com

Alabama Wildlife and Freshwater Fisheries Division
64 Union Street
Montgomery, AL 36130
(334) 242-3465
www.outdooralabama.com

Bear Creek Development Authority
P.O. Box 670
Russellville, AL 35653
(877) 367-2232
www.bearcreeklakes.com

Bon Secour National Wildlife Refuge
12295 Highway 180
Gulf Shores, AL 35603
(251) 540-7720
www.fws.gov/bonsecour

Gulf State Park
22050 Campground Road
Gulf Shore, Al 36542
(251) 948-6353
www.alapark.com

Little River Canyon National Preserve
2141 Gault Avenue North
Fort Payne, AL 35967
(256) 845-9605
www.nps.gov/liri

Outdoor Alabama
Official Web site of Alabama Department of Conservation and Natural Resources
www.outdooralabama.com

Talladega Ranger District
Talladega National Forest
1001 North Street

Talladega, Al 35160
(256) 362-2909
www.fs.fed.us/r8/alabama/forests/talladega_rd/index.shtml
Tennessee Valley Authority
TVA Recreation Areas
400 West Summit Drive WT 11A
Knoxville, TN 37902-1401
www.tva.gov
U.S. Army Corps of Engineers
Army Engineer District, Mobile
P.O. Box 2288
Mobile, AL 36628
(251) 471-5966
www.usace.army.mil
USDA Forest Service, William B. Bankhead District
1070 Highway 33 North
Double Springs, AL 35553
(205) 489-5111
www.fs.fed.us/r8/alabama
Weeks Bay National Estuarine Research Reserve
Alabama Department of Economic and Community Affairs
11300 U.S. Highway 98
Fairhope, AL 36532
(251) 928-9792

Private Sources of Information and/or Equipment

Cahaba River Society
www.cahabariversociety.org.
Coosa River Adventures
415 Company Street
Wetumpka, AL 36092
(334) 514-0279
www.coosariveradventures.com
Flint River Canoe Rentals
107 Michael Drive
Huntsville, AL 35811
(256) 858-2280
Lay Lake Home Owners and Boat Owners Association
P.O. Box 354
Wilsonville, AL 35186
Terrapin Outdoor Center
4114 County Road 175
Piedmont, AL 36272
(256) 447-6666
www.canoeshop.net

Wild Alabama
11312 Highway 33
Moulton, AL 35650
(256) 974-6166
http://content.wildsouth.org/
Fishin.com
www.fishin.com
Provides fishing reports, articles, and information for Alabama, Kentucky, Tennessee, Georgia, Florida, Arkansas, Texas, Illinois, Virginia, South Carolina, North Carolina, and Louisiana.

Chambers of Commerce

Alabama Gulf Coast Area Chamber of Commerce
3150 Gulf Shores Parkway
Gulf Shores, AL 36547
(251) 968-6904
www.alagulfcoastchamber.com
Alabama Mountain Lakes
25062 North Street
Mooresville, AL 35649
(800) 648-5381
www.almtlakes.org
Chamber of Commerce of Huntsville/Madison County
225 Church Street
Huntsville, AL 35804
(256) 535-2000
www.hsvchamber.org
Chilton County Chamber of Commerce
500 Fifth Avenue
Clanton, AL 35046
(800) 553-0419
www.chilton.al.us
Cullman Area Chamber of Commerce
211 Second Avenue NE
P.O. Box 1104
Cullman, AL 35056
www.cullmanchamber.org
Dauphin Island Chamber of Commerce
1011 Bienville Boulevard
Dauphin Island, AL 36528
(877) 532-8744
dauphinisland.cc
Demopolis Chamber of Commerce
102 East Washington Street
P.O. Box 667

Demopolis, AL 36732
www.demopolischamber.com
Enterprise Chamber of Commerce
553 Glover Street
Evergreen, AL 36330
(800) 235-4730
www.enterprisealabama.com
Evergreen/Conecuh County Chamber of Commerce
100 Depot Street
Evergreen, AL 36401
(251) 578-1707
www.enterprisealabama.com
Florala Chamber of Commerce
405 South Fifth Street, Suite 100
Florala, AL 36452
(334) 858-6252
www.fairpoint.net
Huntsville/Madison County Convention and Visitors Bureau
700 Monroe Street
Huntsville, AL 35801
(256) 551-2230
www.huntsville.org
Mobile Chamber of Commerce
P.O. Box 2187
Mobile, AL 36652
(251) 433-6951
www.mobcham.org
Sylacauga Chamber of Commerce
17 Fort Williams
Sylacauga, AL 35150
(256) 249-0308
www.sylacauga.net
Wetumpka Chamber of Commerce
110 East Bridge Street
Wetumpka, AL 36092
(334) 567-4811
www.wetumpkachamber.com
Wilcox Area Chamber of Commerce
110 Court Street
Camden, AL 36726
www.wilcoxareachamber.org

Index

About the Author

Ed Mashburn has fished in many locations, from the streams of the Ozarks and Northern California to the bayous and coastal waters of Florida, Mississippi, and, of course, Alabama. He is text editor and contributing writer for *Florida Sportfishing* and *Destination Fish* magazines. He has also published several articles in *Southern Sporting Journal*. When not fishing or editing, he is an English teacher at Baldwin County High School and adjunct instructor at Faulkner State College in Alabama. In addition to writing about fishing, he has published several magazine articles on gardening and wooden boatbuilding—he can often be found on the waters of coastal Alabama in one of his wooden kayaks in pursuit of redfish.